Heaven, Can You Hear Me?

The New Road to an Extraordinary Life

Kathryn Cormier

Story Mountain Media

Knoxville, Tennessee, USA

www.crippledbeaglepublishing.com

Cover design by Kathryn Cormier

ISBN: 978-1-968830-08-3

Printed in the United States of America

Dedication

I dedicate this writing to these pillars of strength...

Above all, a loving God who knows my innermost self and has shown me His transformative work in me! I am honored and profoundly loved.

Second, to my precious children, Josh and Jylian who endured so much more than they understood as we made it through together.

To my parents, who have faced life's toughest trials with abundant grace and a calm resilience that inspires me daily.

To my brother, Tommy, who taught me how to stand up and confront my battles, my personal "Vietnam." I am eternally thankful for the depth of his care and love for me.

To my sister, Joan, who accepted my phone calls where I

couldn't form a word, the sobs were so deep. She exemplified the unwavering strength of Christ's love.

And to my dear attorneys and other friends and family members who helped with the heavy lifting of a false accusation that many days crushed my spirit.

I am forever grateful.

In perfect love,

Kathy

What Day Is It?

My mind was reeling. I thought I heard him say, "Innocent people go to jail all the time. You guys need to make arrangements for someone to raise your kids . . . just in case." This was advice from our close friend who is an attorney and was best man at our wedding.

Indictment? What on earth is an indictment? "Charged with felonious sexual assault of two minor children thirty-three and a half years' imprisonment" went past my ears, but I didn't comprehend it. It was as though I had moved to another country and didn't speak their language. I was petrified of something I didn't understand. I had no idea how much danger I was in. Please, I thought, tell me where my kids are. . . .

Sometimes, in life, we experience deep, painful hardships and must desperately work to get on our feet again. I was in the process of a divorce after a ten-year marriage with two little ones in tow. The pain and disappointment of a perceived failed life were palpable every day. The numbing of the unknown responsibilities and unrelenting stress of making it through another twenty-four hours felt unbearable. You think you're on track and you're gonna make it okay . . . and then this (whatever your *this* is) happens . . . and you think again.

Chapter One

Echoes of Intent

My personality born into this human existence is one of great curiosity and what I call phenomenology! My husband used to call me a phenomenologist—so I own it! I seek the mysteries in life and the uncanny "coincidences" (of which I believe there are none—all is intentional). They light me up when they just align themselves, and all for the common good! However, within this human experience, while embracing many joys, big and small, no one is exempt from experiencing challenges, hardships, losses, failures, and discomforts, and I want to be clear from the beginning that I am well aware of this as you will learn in this book.

I have a hummingbird feeder in my backyard not far from the patio. This morning as I sat at my desk writing, there were four beautiful hummingbirds flitting around the bright-red glass feeder hanging from the garden hook. They are such remarkable creatures, and did you know they are the smallest known living dinosaur? I did not! Last night, one hovered right in front of my face. Because I was very surprised that it came so close, I stayed really still, just loving the sound of his wings and admiring the many gorgeous colors of his feathers. Like the cardinal, the male gets the beautiful colors in his wings.

He also made this sweet chirping sound. I had never heard it before, and it was so unique. It made me think how this tiny, tiny creature is continually cared for and provided for its entire life span. While instinctively aware of predators, it knows the potential dangers around it but finds its food for the day and exists in all its glory. It possesses a fragment of the capacity of thinking ability that I have as a human being. What if I applied the same awe every day to my far greater, deeply inspired, intellectual, wonderfully made physical body, and above all spiritual capacity allotted to my years in this life when those challenges show up? Could just thinking about them differently affect the impact and outcomes?

Today, you are cordially invited into my life. The good, the bad and the "wow"! Why on earth would you want to know—or care—about my life? There are millions upon millions of biographies and autobiographies out there that want to shine light into your psyche, impact your value system, and challenge your belief system. Is this just another one of those, you ask? It may be—or it may not—but I can tell you that it is mine, and it will prove to show how the experiences in my life have touched hundreds, if not thousands, of other lives in profound ways in which I had no intentional part in the orchestration. See, I believe that we all impact many, many lives every day—unknowingly. I hope this inspires you to contemplate how your life is influencing the ones placed in your path. Here goes. . . .

Molding Convictions

I met Craig when I was nineteen and very inexperienced and truly naive. I had been on maybe five dates up until that time. I was not the kid who ran around with the crowd, nor was I found in places I shouldn't have been. My sister, Susan, was living in Michigan at the time, and my parents traveled out to visit her and her family. When they returned from that trip, my dad said to me, "I met the man you're going to marry." I was intrigued! I had always wondered who and when that someone special would come along for me. It was great that Craig was coming to me at the suggestion of my dad because Dad was my hero. I was and still am a daddy's girl. I have loved my relationship with him my whole life.

A few months later, on a cold, wintery day in February 1976, I took my very first flight from Boston to Grand Rapids, Michigan, to "visit my sister" and check out this newfound hot stuff my dad had told me about, and I met Craig for the first time. Funny thing: Susan had my high school graduation picture on a shelf in her living room, and one day when Craig had come by to visit them, he asked, "Who's that?" She told him, "My sister." He said he would like to meet me if I came to visit. When he came to the door, he had hair down to his shoulders, he had a lit cigarette in his hand, and I believe he was high. I laughed to myself, thinking, "Okay, Dad, I'll go with it!"

We were quite taken with each other, and that began a long-distance relationship for about eight months.

I remember pining away in our recreation room downstairs in our home on Lincoln Street Extension in Natick,

Massachusetts. During those long, lonely evenings, I would find myself playing the same five or ten 45-RPM records most every evening that spoke the feelings within my young heart: "Precious and Few," "I'd Really Love To See You Tonight," and so many others. I'd be singing at the top of my lungs! I played every Carole King song on my sister's albums, just waiting for the day to come when I would fly to Michigan or he would fly to Boston and we would be together again.

We flew back and forth about every six weeks to see each other, and in October that year, I moved to Michigan and lived with his Aunt Vada as a roommate in her spare bedroom. She was an absolute love!

Prior to my move to Michigan, Craig had a job in radio and TV repair in Kalkaska, and at the time, I was working in administration at the local hospital in Natick. Our decision for me to move was based on the fact that it would have been easier for me to find a job there than for him to find his work in the Boston area. So off I went, leaving home for the first time and moving very far away from everything I had ever known.

I found a job pretty quickly at a manufacturing plant called Craft House where they manufactured paint-by-number kits, and I worked in the office and became their receptionist. I really liked the job and loved the people I worked with at Craft House.

I graduated early from Natick High School in 1975. During my high school years, I worked in a medical library at Leonard Morse Hospital. I was then hired to be secretary to the executive committee and office manager for employee health at the same time. I stayed in these positions until moving to Michigan.

I didn't like school—almost ever! I couldn't wait to get out. I didn't go to prom and graduated early in January to just get out and get to work. I literally stayed home a minimum of thirty days a year through my school years, and Mom would let me! Best part!

After living in Kalkaska just short of a year, Craig and I decided to move back east to the beautiful White Mountains of New Hampshire. Craig's childhood happened in that tiny town of Kalkaska, and he didn't think he could handle the busy city of Boston where most of my family resided. My three older brothers, at this time, had a rising country rock band, and they, along with their families, lived in North Conway, New Hampshire, so living there became the compromise of where to land. We had a few different jobs. He worked at one of the ski resorts running ski lifts, and I worked some secretarial positions.

Craig lived with my brother and his family, and I lived in a little two-room apartment just up the street. It was on the third floor, so groceries and laundry were always interesting and kept me fit!

One Sunday afternoon, when we had been dating for two and a half years, we were in my apartment and I brought up getting married (yet again). He agreed or caved—I'm not sure which, honestly. The wedding was set for June 18, 1978. It was Father's Day that year. It was a way to include his dad, who had now been gone for several years. We were married in my parents' backyard under a trellis, and the ceremony was officiated by a female justice of the peace. We couldn't find a priest or clergyman who would come to the house and marry us outdoors in the backyard. Things change! There were a lot of people at the wedding because my family is large. A few friends and his family came from Michigan. I was twenty-one and he was twenty-two. His friend, Kim, stood up for him, and my sister stood up for me.

We lived in that little apartment in Conway, New Hampshire, for about a year and then had the wonderful opportunity to buy land and build our first home on East Conway Road! It was a little brown Cape Cod style with only the first floor finished. We worked together to clear the land on our time off. We cut up all the trees and stacked firewood to use in the woodstoves. It was really fun setting up our little home in the woods. I was into crafting at the time, and he loved to work with wood in the basement workshop. He made our end tables for the living room, and I stenciled walls and hung curtains after we painted walls the beige colors of the time!

Craig eventually found a position in his field of radio and TV repair in a little shop in Center Conway. I worked in administrative roles in a law firm and at one point for an insurance agency, then eventually I also enjoyed working for Country Squire Real Estate as a receptionist and assistant to the office manager.

Our marriage had a pretty rough start because I got pregnant on our honeymoon (unknowingly) and proceeded to have female trouble over the next two months. Doctors missed what was happening, and each would tell me that "it was the newness of marriage!" What the heck? I thought to myself, "If this keeps up, I'm heading back to singleness in short order!"

On September 13, 1978, I went to work like any other day, but this day, I was feeling pretty exhausted. Craig and I drove to and from work together at that time because we worked right next door to each other. At five o'clock, I got in the car, and as he started to drive home, I started to faint. I put my head down to my lap, and if I sat up, I lost consciousness. He drove directly to Tom and Chris's house, wondering what the heck was going on! He and Tom helped me walk into the house, supporting me on each side. I remember walking, but I was blacked out at the same time. We spent the night there, and I was in excruciating pain in my abdomen and couldn't take a deep breath or sit up without passing out. Christine called the emergency room and told them what was happening, and they said it sounded like a stomach virus and they would call in Paregoric for me. Paragoric was an over-the-counter medicine used way back in the early 18th century and still today for stomach ailments. I guess it contained opium and it helped with pain. I remember as a child having it by the teaspoon for stomach trouble!

Lord, I know what you are thinking right now. As I tell this story, it makes me shudder! Well, the next day I wasn't any better, so they called an ambulance, and off I went to the emergency room.

A young, brand-new Dr. Ray Rabideau, about twenty-eight years old, came into the examining room. I was his very first patient in his very new practice.

In July and August, I saw Dr. Hope. He was a primary-care doctor who delivered babies and practiced in a little town just south of Conway. At the time of my visit, he was out of pregnancy tests, so he missed it. He did think I may have miscarried the month before, however, because of the way things were looking physically, so I left his office thinking that was the truth and just went on.

In the emergency room, Dr. Rabideau announced, "You're pregnant." I said, "That's not possible. Dr. Hope thought I had miscarried last month." Well, tests don't lie. Ray was very concerned about my continuing to pass out. It most likely meant I was losing blood somewhere, yet there were no external indicators of that. Ray was not a surgeon, and this was a tiny town hospital. The only gynecologist on staff was a Dr. Paret. Ray needed to get him involved. He showed Dr. Paret the test results that showed I was pregnant and said he suspected an ectopic pregnancy. Paret disagreed and thought I had a stomach virus. He refused to do the laparoscopy to determine what was going on. I was admitted to the hospital because of not being able to stay conscious. My friend Brenda was Ray's secretary at the time, and she later told me that he came back to the office, sat back in his chair, and said, "She is going to die and I can't do a damn thing about it." He then did one more test. It involved a long needle inserted into the lining of my uterus. If the fluid came back clear, I was not bleeding internally. If it was filled with blood, then I was in serious trouble. So he took the syringe full of blood and put it in the mailbox of Dr. Paret, then said, "I just drew this out of the patient you think has a stomach virus." Ray was really struggling to get Paret to do the right thing.

I was given three pints of blood. At midnight, I woke up with the doctors standing on either side of my bed—that was the weirdest feeling ever. Ray said, "Kathy, your hemoglobin levels have dropped again, so we are going to do surgery in the morning."

Oh my gosh, I forgot the funniest thing that happened that day. Kind of funny—bear with my sense of humor!

I was admitted to a room with an older woman with a heart condition. They put me in the bed, we said hello, and I was so exhausted, I tried to fall asleep. Well, after a little while—I don't really know how long—I had to go to the bathroom. So without thinking (I was twenty-one, remember), I climbed out of the bed on the closet side of the bed. I took one step and proceeded to fall backwards into the closet and passed out. The last thing I remember hearing was that woman with a heart condition screaming, "Help! Help!" The next thing I knew, I had two orderlies picking me up by my arms and putting me back in the bed. I don't know what happened next about going to the bathroom, but I do remember Ray sitting on the bed when I came to, and he ordered blood for me and asked me not to get up again without help! LOL! I don't really know what happened to the woman with the heart condition. But she sure could scream HELP!

At nine o'clock the next morning, I was in surgery. Ray was a general practitioner, but he gowned up and went in to observe. Honestly, I think he was really scared to let Paret touch me.

Craig waited anxiously outside the operating room for my progress update. He said when Dr. Paret came out of surgery, his hands were shaking, and he was as white as a ghost. They told him I had had an ectopic pregnancy, and they removed my left fallopian tube. Ray said the fetus was about six weeks' gestation and that they would send it away for pathology. I never learned anything about the results of that. They were able to leave the ovary, but when they did the laparoscopy, the blood shot out like a water fountain.

Healing from this ordeal was long and arduous. I was cut wide open over six inches long from my navel. I was out of work for three weeks, and it was very slow going back. I was told it would take several months for my body to replenish the blood I had lost and was instructed to not push and give myself time to heal. My body went into a deep, physical depression that winter, and in February of the next year, I sat on the bank of the Saco River considering the unthinkable. Jeepers, all I did was get married! I was a young, inexperienced virgin girl, and I didn't know half of what was happening to me. I had been within twenty-four hours of dying, according to Dr. Rabideau. God was there for me in spite of the circumstances. I had a doctor who really cared about his first patient. I will forever be thankful to him. He saved my life!

My parents lived in the Boston area at the time about three hours south, so they weren't able to come up until the next day. They still had my four younger brothers at home, and it wasn't easy to just jump in the car and go. I know they were worried.

I returned to work in February 1979 for a local attorney as a paralegal/administrative assistant. I worked there for about six months, and then I worked for Country Squire Real Estate. I loved working there. After some time, I knew there was more that I should do with my life, so I looked into beginning a home-based day care. I absolutely love children, and I am a natural with them.

Craig was reluctant to take the leap because of finances, but I knew I could make a go of it and fulfill my purpose in life. I thought at eighteen, coming out of high school, that working in secretarial or administrative work was all that I could do. I didn't learn how to dream—how to consider options. I really just remember following—following in someone else's footsteps, like my two older sisters. They both were in those roles for their occupations. I was physically ill—a lot—in most of those jobs. Funny how our bodies will tell us where and what and how we should be expressing ourselves in this life.

My wonderful life of coaching has pulled all the correct pieces together for me. I find my spirit reaching, stretching, expanding into a realm of giving like I've never experienced before. Have you felt that in your life, too? Do you see where you contribute, help, or give to others' lives in your occupation and yet still feel a sense of contracting or even "extracting" valuable energy from your very being? There is a purpose for your life. Yes, your life—your very existence—has been designed to participate in life and contribute to life like no other human being can! Isn't that the most wonderful news? I felt this longing and discontent in my life at a very young age and kept seeking the answers. I can only see this through the lens and framework of looking back over many years. They say hindsight is 20/20. No truer words. What is your longing and discontent today? Is it the same as when you were eighteen? Is it different? How so?

Chapter Two

In January 1981, I took the plunge! I gave my two-week notice at Country Squire Real Estate and began to repurpose the bedroom on the first level while Craig worked to finish off our upstairs into two bedrooms. Our home provided lots of outdoor space to play and plant a garden. I put a small ad in the paper and told some friends, and in no time I was up and running. My first little girl was the sweetest thing you could imagine. I loved her parents immediately, and she began the line-up at the door. I was licensed by the state pretty quickly, and I hired my cousin, Jean, to help me on the heavy days! We had a ball together.

Craig, meanwhile, had moved toward opening his own business in North Conway doing radio and TV repair. Mountain Village TV became a successful repair shop in town. He had a dark blue van that had a snazzy business wrap all around it. People in town knew who he was when that van made its way down the road. He was really skilled at what he did. He could fix anything electronic, and he worked hard. He was the guy you could rely on showing up when he said he was going to be there.

He was a volunteer fireman and a first responder as well. That work really interested him.

We eventually added movie video rentals to the shop. We were one of the first to do so in town—back when that was a thing! My, how times have changed! We chose not to carry X-rated films because doing so would not align with our core values. We also branched into the home satellite business as well. He was a one-stop shop!

When he was a kid, Craig's dad sold municipal water pipelines to towns and cities. He was on the road all week through most of Craig's childhood and was home on the weekends. They would work on ham radios together on the weekends and enjoyed that hobby. Craig had two older sisters and was pretty close to his family and extended family in Michigan. Sadly, his dad's health paid dearly for the life of driving long distances and living a life on the road. He had his first heart attack very young and passed in his forties just a year before Craig and I met. His dad was one of the very first people in the country to have had a heart bypass procedure done by the internationally known cardiologist and pioneer Dr. Michael DeBakey. His dad had had several serious heart attacks at a young age. Apparently, he was a good candidate for the bypass surgery, and it ultimately extended his life by five years. He passed from a final heart attack when Craig was in college and eighteen years old.

I had never lost anyone very close to me, and we discussed his dad often because he was still dealing with the deep loss of him. During our twelve years together, I don't think he ever really got over that loss.

The day-care business was a great success, and lo and behold, about two months into it, I found out I was pregnant. Joshua Craig was a miracle baby after the ectopic pregnancy damage. After a short break to figure out how to get any sleep with this little munchkin and how I was going to reopen the day care, I had five little five-month-old babies at one time in the day care. One was Josh, and they all became fast friends! Over the course of two and a half years, seventy-two children, mostly under six years old, went through my care. I had a great preschool program that helped them learn their letters and numbers, and we had lots of playtime and music and dancing. It was great fun! Sesame Street and Mr. Rogers Neighborhood were daily staples and the only TV watching they had as I prepared their lunch. I loved those shows!

The days were so busy and full of energy. We would have something planned for an activity in the morning, and they would have a snack together at about 9 a.m. Lunch would be at 11:30, and we had quiet time/naptime for an hour sometime between 12 and 1 most days. We had three cribs upstairs in Josh's bedroom for my sleeping babies. We would get the bottle feeders done, change diapers, and put the babies down for their naps as needed. Some napped both morning and afternoon, depending on their schedules. After lunch, the older children would line up for potty time or diaper changes, wash their hands, and lay on their mats in the playroom. I would put on lullaby music and pull the shades, and soon most of them would be sound asleep. Whatever one did, the others would follow. I rarely had a child who didn't fall asleep. Those not wanting to sleep would need to be quiet while their playmates were napping, so why wouldn't they just fall asleep? Right?

After nap, we had free-time play in the playroom. If the weather permitted, we were outside every day for some part of the day. They loved playing in the sand and roaming around the backyard and following me on a nature treasure hunt in the woods in the back. That outdoor walk would provide so many things to talk about! The fall would give us beautiful leaves of so many colors as New England is so well known for! We could do lots of projects with them. The pine cones in the woods gave us ideas around Christmastime, and they loved taking the "hats" off the acorns!

Pickup time was always the challenge. It's a funny, short period of time where the child questions who is in charge—me or their mom or dad. So while the parent and I are talking, bar none, that child will run around and do all the things they know they are not supposed to do—like run on the furniture, hit another kid on the head, throw a toy. It was the strangest thing! So I knew that the chitchat needed to be short on the pickup or something bad was about to happen! "Here's your hat—what's your hurry?"

I spent many evenings and even some weekends developing strategies and activities for the kids to learn some new skill or song or game. One thing I know for sure: while you are "raising" kids, you can't cut corners and win. I loved these little people like they were my own. I felt responsible for them learning new things in the same way I did for Josh.

It's a funny thing sometimes in life when we try to "be efficient" or "cut corners" and have such different results. I remember in my own family we always had chores for the kids growing up. I think it makes children feel like they are needed and an important part of the thing we call family. They may hem and haw over it, but it instills responsibility and promotes character and integrity.

While raising my own family, at one time we had a bird named Sunny, a cockatiel, who was gray and white with this beautiful orange in his cheeks. Well, at least we think he was a he. We found an egg in his cage one day. There was never another bird with "him," so it raised a lot of curiosity at the time. I really don't remember if we actually figured it out, but I do remember the egg! Well, it was my daughter's job that day to clean his cage. The cage was white metal, and the bottom detached from the upper cage part so you could leave Sunny in the cage while cleaning him up and he wouldn't escape. Jylian thought it would be a good idea to take Sunny out of the cage and let him walk around on her shoulders while she used the vacuum hose to suck up all the sunflower shells and change out the paper towels on the base of the cage. I was working in the next room in the kitchen preparing supper, and she was in the den, and all of a sudden I heard screaming: "Shut it off! Shut it off!" along with the loud whir of the vacuum. I turn to run to the room, and as I come through the doorway, there she is with the top of the vacuum hose and Sunny is head-first in the hose. His wings are flapping like a madman trying to keep from being sucked into the vacuum.

I ran over to the plug and quickly pulled it from the wall. When I turned and looked back as the whir of the vacuum slowly stopped, I saw Sunny pulling his head out of the top of the vacuum hose. His plume was standing straight up on top of his head like a bad day of Elvis in the wind. His eyes were going cuckoo, and the look on his face was like "I don't know where I just was, but I sure as heck know I don't ever want to go back there again!" I turned to Jyl and said, "What in the world were you doing?" She was so upset and shaking. She said, "I was vacuuming up the seeds and Sunny was on my shoulder, and he turned around and I saw this pinfeather hanging off the back of him, so I thought I would vacuum it. He turned around fast and he went head-first into the hose!"

Now . . . please, all my animal lovers, don't hate me. I love animals. I loved Sunny. I also have a sense of humor developed from a comical father and had nine very funny siblings. Since Sunny was okay (I believe), it took everything in my being not to absolutely ga-haw right then and there! I kissed Jyl on the head and said, "Maybe we won't choose that again in the future." I got up, left the room, and silently laughed around the corner till I nearly wet myself.

Using the vacuum to grab the feather might have been cutting a corner instead of just pulling it out and may have spared the bird many years of PTSD. As far as Sunny was concerned, from that day forward, I would sing when I cleaned the house, as usual, and he would be in the guest bedroom just squawking loud and clear—singing along with me. But as soon as I turned on the vacuum cleaner, he changed his tune in a big way! The squawk was in a high pitch from another stratosphere. Don't worry, he was always safe in his cage. . . .

This is a story I share pretty often, and every time it just brings me right back to that room. I can see the color of the walls, the sun streaming through the front windows, the color of the carpet and how the toy boxes were built into the closet. I hear Jyl's voice and see her little blonde head as she sits there on the floor. It's one of many stories I treasure in my heart, gathered from raising four of them. I love being a parent. I love even more being a grandparent. The amazing miracles of how life begins and ends are my favorite phenomena! I feel it is a great privilege to be graced with the opportunity to know and to love both the young and the old. Oh, I love the in-betweens, too, but there is something special about the beginning and the end.

Have you ever watched a little three- or four-month-old baby notice their hand for the first time? How they move it around in front of their vision as if to say, "Now what on earth is this thing?" Then they figure out it punches them in the eye or fills up their mouth, where tender gums will chew and teethe on that little fist. Then shortly after that, they reach for that toy floating on that mobile above their head. They might soothe themselves by sucking their thumb or fingers. Just to watch their little eyes discover their body is wicked cool—as we say in Boston.

We come into this world completely helpless and dependent on our every need. We have just survived potentially the most dangerous passage of our entire life just getting here. Medically speaking, the birthing process remains one of the most critical and vulnerable times in a child's life. That's quite a lot to say about a little bundle of mighty, incredible, dependent life source with a unique, one-of-a-kind soul. Many of us have lived twenty, thirty, forty, or more years on this blue marble.

Imagine what this tiny little creature is about to achieve in a very short five years. How much that brain expands and learns—rolling, eating, drinking, creeping; crying when hungry, sad, or not feeling well; crawling, smiling, connecting, recognizing, walking, falling down, playing, to name just a few! They grow exponentially, doubling in size, over and over, right before our eyes, and yet we don't see it. And we fall deeply in love with this little human being and spirit, entrusted to us for their time here. How very fortunate and blessed we are. And I think, "Why this one? Why me?" I just love it so much.

The same holds true for your grandchildren, foster children, bonus children, adopted children: "Why this one? Why me?" So enormously grateful! It is my greatest privilege in the human experience. What does it mean to you? If you were not asked to know children in this way, in what way have you been called to impact the lives of children in your world? We all are touched by a child along the way. They remind us of maintaining an innocent life along the road. They teach us how to care for others and how to project our true "self" before the world gets a hold of us.

There is a beautiful verse in the Bible in Matthew 18:3 that reads, "Truly, I tell you, unless you change and become like little children, you will never enter the kingdom of heaven." This verse emphasizes the qualities of humility, trust, and innocence that children embody. Jesus uses a child as a powerful symbol of innocence and dependence, contrasting it with the often prideful and self-sufficient attitudes that adults can develop. I wonder what would happen if today, right now, you and I were to embrace a sense of wonder, curiosity, and simplicity such as those of a child, allowing ourselves to experience spirituality with a fresh perspective. How far off the road am I? Are you? This is a learning curve we don't want to cut.

Chapter Three

Change was a-comin'. . .

Although I loved what I was doing in the day care, when our little man Josh turned two, he was having a struggle sharing Mom with all these kids all day long. I didn't have a lap much, unless I was sprawled out on the floor and all the kids were crawling all over me like ants on an anthill. My cousin Jeannie would have her bunch doing the same thing. I had to make a difficult decision and close the child care. Craig needed extra hands at the shop, so that's where I went to work. I'll never forget that when I had to tell all my families, which just killed me, one of the little boys, Seth, told his mom that he couldn't go to my house anymore because I loved Josh more than the other kids. He was hurt and felt slighted. He didn't see Josh as my son. To him, Josh was just one of the other kids. They each truly mattered to me. I felt so sad about Seth!

Thankfully, one of the moms from my day care decided to grab the baton and started her own in-home day care. We enrolled Josh there with MaryJo two days a week. Quite a few of the other families followed suit. His little friends were there as well, and it was working out nicely! A short while later, I discovered that I was pregnant again. The baby was due in November of that year, 1986.

Sometime in 1982, while Josh was still a baby, I was invited to a Discovery Toys home demonstration. Discovery Toys is a multilevel marketing company that sells high-quality, educational toys, books, and games from all over the world! I thought, well, I could surely use these for all my kids in the day care, and I fell in love with them! It was a great side-hustle to my day care business, so I became an educational consultant for the company. As a secondary business, I did demos all over the place and became pretty successful at it. I was the only consultant initially for a one hundred-mile radius! It was a salesperson's playground!

Over time, because the company was designed as a multilevel marketing company, I eventually recruited other consultants who then recruited others, and so on. I had sixty-eight people selling under me. I absolutely loved teaching the children through the Discovery Toys products during the days and teaching parents in the evenings and on weekends how to use them with their kids at home—it was a complete win! I equally loved the lifelong friendships I developed with the other educational consultants who joined me on the journey. The money was great, and I earned their incentive trip each year! We were able to travel to places like Hawaii, London, Paris, Punta Cana, and the Bahamas. These opportunities existed only in our dreams, so it was really great and lots of fun!

In November 1986, along came Jylian Kate, another

miracle baby. Her name was chosen from a character I watched on Ryan's Hope—a soap opera! LOL! The actress spelled her name Gillian! We started out that way until the day she was born and the pediatrician came in and looked down at her and said, "Hi, Gillian" with a hard g—like Gilligan! Well, that was it for that spelling! Then we thought about Jillian—but that looked like Jill with too many letters. So we spelled it Jylian—that way there wouldn't be any confusion all her life. Her name also is a combination of my parents' names—George and Lillian! I was so happy Josh would have a sibling and not be an only child. My life became very busy! Our marriage was struggling, and I knew Craig was not happy in his life. He had become very withdrawn and distant. It was becoming evident that he wanted out, and I was scared to death.

So far you've learned about just ten years of our lives. A lot happens in a short period of time, doesn't it? Can you take just ten years of your life and make a written inventory of happenings in your life? Word has it that life is short. That time flies. I know you will periodically notice how much the dog has grown or how your parents have aged. We ask or sing, "Who Knows Where the Time Goes?" Time is only present in this human dimension. I love how time is measured in twenty-four-hour increments. This twenty-four-hour increment, today, has never been, and at midnight tonight, it will never be again. Think on that for a minute: we have a brand new start every twenty-four hours. So if this one day isn't going too well, wait. It will end . . . and you will begin again. You won't be the same person physically tomorrow that you are today. Your cells in your body are always changing, replacing. Ever wonder who or what breathes you while you sleep? Ever wonder who or what keeps your heart beating all day while you go about your business? Ever wonder why your liver will grow itself back but your pancreas won't? Ever wonder why the cornea in your eye will grow back within seventy-two hours but your retina won't? You don't do any of that—some greater power or energy or being does that for us. Phenomenal, right?

I call this power God; you call it what you call it: spirit, infinite intelligence, universe, et cetera. I have always felt the presence of God in my life. Looking back, even before I learned about Him, I know I have always sensed His presence.

Reading what you have read so far has set the stage for this next set of circumstances, situations, and conditions that I believe occurred on another level of life. It was, bar none, one of the most difficult, painful, frightening, life-threatening, humiliating times that one should ever endure. Here we go… Hang in there because the phenomena will follow . . . I promise. . . .

Chapter Four

The First Rumble…

The 1980s witch hunt is a term used to describe the moral panic that occurred in the 1980s and early 1990s, when day-care providers were accused of child abuse, including Satanic ritual abuses. These cases are often considered part of the Satanic Panic, which is a collection of over 12,000 unsubstantiated cases of Satanic ritual abuse. The Satanic Panic has spread around the world and continues today. Constructed and promulgated by journalists, prosecuting attorneys, "academics," and "expert witnesses," the witch-hunt narrative argues that a kind of mass hysteria overtook the country in the 1980s, leading to hundreds of false and outlandish accusations and widespread convictions of innocents.

My heart breaks sharing that bit of history because my life has always demonstrated being a passionate advocate for the voice of children who have been abused in any way. I abhor the enormous atrocities of the many abuses children are subjected to in our world, both today and throughout this country's past. I blindly wanted to trust our judicial system and feel secure within its jurisdiction. I wanted to believe that only the bad guys are caught and rightfully prosecuted to the full extent of the law and that children will always be protected from harm. In my naivety at thirty years old, I believed these things to be true.

Here is where the year of tribulation begins. . . .

January and February were cold, cold, cold in the Northeast! We had a new baby, and Josh was loving his preschool and his little friends so much. He was the best boy and smart as a whip. Craig and I both loved being parents. We actually worked together like a fine-greased machine, and things at home and at the business got done. We are both very responsible people by nature, but there was no longer any emotional connection. That had been the case for a very long time. We really had been blessed with an adorable little Cape Cod house on a sweet piece of land. We had work and success and two healthy kids. I think that our staying together as a couple was more by default than by design. One of those things where you think, "Well, we have been together this long; why start over?" It's as though after dating for over two years, marrying would just be the next expected thing to happen, right? Not so, I believe that fear can skew our capacity to logically make decisions. When we don't use brave thinking, results in our lives will reflect and expose the avoidance of truth. On March 18, 1987, Craig came home very late. We were supposed to be at a friend's home for a party that evening, and he was out drinking and came home drunk. I knew then we were not going anywhere. He took

Josh, then four years old, into the bathroom, and I went upstairs to put Jylian, then four months old, down to sleep. I was seriously annoyed. I heard a loud crash and came downstairs. Josh was crying. Evidently, while Craig had been holding him, Josh had pushed Craig on his shoulders. Craig lost his balance and fell back into the tub, and the shower curtain came down and hit Josh on the head. They came out of the bathroom and into the kitchen and Josh said, "Mommy, Daddy isn't gonna live with us anymore." Now, both annoyed and puzzled, I asked, "What? What do you mean, honey?" Then it gets kinda fuzzy. He told our four-year-old son, before he told me, that he was leaving. I was livid.

Josh went up to bed, and when Craig came down, we talked briefly in the playroom. He apologized through drunken tears and said he didn't want to be married anymore. Then he got up and left. In the stillness of that evening that followed, sitting in the dark, I remember thinking, "I am thirty years old, I've got a four-year-old son who worships his dad, and I'm still nursing a four-month-old baby girl." I also realized that I would then proceed to lose my employment, because my working with him at the TV shop obviously wouldn't continue. What would happen now? I cried out of frustration, fear, disillusionment, and downright shock.

Twelve years together. He was the only man I had ever known in a long-term relationship. I was so scared, broken, defeated, confused, and disappointed. What was I going to do now to make a living? How would I help my tiny, sensitive, broken boy heal? That was the hardest thing of all. Over the nights that followed, as I tucked him into bed,

Josh always wanted to talk about his day. Those conversations changed to wiping tears and sharing how he was planning to burn down all the houses in the whole world so Daddy would have to live in our house. Or then asking, "Mom, can we build another house in the back for Daddy to live in so he will be close?" He was four. It was gut-wrenching! I had no words.

Josh would never have the same look in his eyes after the night Craig left. All his photos showed the pain. He tried to cover it up. It showed in his behavior being loud and silly. It hurt too much for him to face. Children never dream of a scenario in which their parents are anywhere but near to them.

Honestly, I had not been happy in our marriage for some time. Craig had checked out emotionally a long time before, and his drinking was like living with "the other woman" in the house all the time. You can't compete with that. I had always hoped that somehow we would find a way, through therapy, revelation, something. But that didn't happen. You can't call all the shots in life. You can't predict the choices that your spouse or partner will make for themselves. It's all part of the risk of loving and committing to another. We tried therapy for a while after Josh was born. Craig didn't want to be married. Again, I didn't know what to do with that and continued to internalize the rejection as meaning something was wrong with me. We went to marriage counseling, and he came back into the marriage and we were okay for a while longer. We just lived more like roommates, I guess. Then, after Jylian was born, it happened at about the four-month mark again. I thought it was some kind of pattern with him after our children were born.

But this time it was for good.

Jylian never knew us living together. She grew up from the start in a single-parent home. In the beginning, Craig would take Josh alone for visitation because Jylian was so small. She was nine months old by the time she actually went with her daddy overnight.

Pain comes in many shapes and sizes. Alcohol and other substances all too often are covering up unresolved emotions and pain. Like disease, pain holds no prisoners. We were young and had no real wisdom to draw from. My emotional love tank was a vast wasteland—alternating between being completely numb and being enraged.

I made up my mind then and there that I would stay in our home with the kids and make some way to afford it. Craig had moved into the shop temporarily and then found a small house to rent with a roommate.

Because I was still nursing, I thought I needed to find a way to work from home, so I thought I would reopen my day-care center. My mom and dad lived locally, so I talked with them about it. My dad, a contractor, said he would retrofit my basement into a day-care area so the business could have separate space from my living area for the sake of my kids.

Dad worked hard to put down indoor/outdoor carpet, sheetrocked the walls and the ceiling, and cleverly built in a really great area that had a half-wall that would serve as a large playpen to keep the babies contained and safe with their age-appropriate toys. It was a perfect space, and I was so grateful to him and my brothers who helped. My mom knew I was really stressed and tired, so she opted to work at the day care with me. I welcomed the help while I figured out this new life I had to do. I continued the Discovery Toys business on nights and weekends. When word got out that I was reopening the doors to the day care, I had thirteen families right away, and I was grateful again. Craig maintained the TV shop, and he was very good about paying child support and stayed loyal to the kids. I was really grateful for that, too. It was very rough emotionally; I remember looking for his truck wherever I would go so I wouldn't run into him with one of his girlfriends. It was more than I could handle.

This was May 1987. I had reached out to Thurlowe Rowe, the state representative who would do the licensing visits for home child-care centers. He and I had a good working relationship the first time I was in business, so I knew he would help me get started again. I called regularly to the state through May, June, and July. Every time I called, they told me they were swamped and they would get to me; I just had to hang on. So I did. I was waiting to expand to more children as was allowable with Mom and I working there together. August came—still no visit.

Still Wondering Why…

Then on August 31, Thurlowe showed up. Finally! I took him through the house and downstairs to see Dad's wonderful work and then back upstairs. Thurlowe was a man of few words, a quiet soul but kind. I said, "Well, what else do you need from me, Thurlowe?"

He paused and then he said, "Well, Kathy, I wish I was here to renew your license, but I've actually come to shut you down."

I said, "Very funny, Thurlowe! I wish I had a better sense of humor about me right now, but, you know . . ."

He smiled and said, "I wish I was kidding, but I'm not. There has been a complaint placed against you at the state level. Until we get those answers resolved, I'm afraid you will have to shut down."

I froze and turned toward him because I didn't believe what I was hearing. The look on his face said it all—I knew then he wasn't kidding. Bewildered, I said, "Who? What?"

He turned to me and said, "I'm afraid I can't tell you that. I will let you know right away once we have it figured out. I'm really sorry, Kathy." He turned toward the door, and he was gone.

I stood there, again just stunned. Now what? I was immediately hurt that someone would be unhappy with my care. Seventy-two kids had gone through my care, and I had never had a complaint or had a child leave because they were unhappy. I was good at what I did, and I knew it.

At this time, New Hampshire law stated that you could have three families in a day care without a license, so I was able to keep three families of my current thirteen. The question was whether I should. Would it be profitable? Would Mom still be able to help? How on earth would I be able to choose from the thirteen families? I loved them all.

A meeting was called. They all came the next night, and I broke the news to them. Remember now, I didn't know if the complaint was from one of them since I had reopened my child care or if it was from someone from three years ago. I might have been staring into the eyes of my accuser—I did not know. I thought I was completely out of tears, but I was wrong. The parents were so shocked and sad that they had to find other care, and because I didn't know how long it would take, I could make no promises. Three families stayed, and Mom stayed on to help.

North Conway, New Hampshire, is one of the most beautiful little towns in New England. It is at the base of five major ski areas, and the majestic Mt. Washington towers over the village with its snowy white peak and beautiful snow caps over the adjacent mountain range. We spent many a weekend hiking those trails and sledding down the mountain roads and laughing until we wet ourselves. It was always the best when it was a full moon and we hiked up the white, unplowed roads and sledded down in the moonlight. It was a scary surprise to come flying around the corner and see the "Snowcat," a gigantic plow with tank treads, making its way to the top of Mt. Washington. I thought we surely would die, but no—we must have had nine lives like cats!

Winters were long and really cold, but it grew on you, and the road crews were amazing! We could have twelve inches of snow overnight and school would happen the next day. If it wasn't icy, we traveled. The community had no more than 10,000 residents, and that included the second-home folks who came and went during the ski season. Cross-country skiing was a favorite through the miles of groomed trails. If the wax was just right under the skis, you could hear the crunch and swoosh through the woods. Snow was just part of our life there. Part of the kids' physical education included skiing on Mt. Cranmore, where they became excellent skiers and snowboarders! Most everyone knew everyone, and your neighbors were not strangers.

Josh had a best friend, Sam, just up the road a little bit, and they played together every day. Sam's mom and dad were a source of comfort and encouragement for me during this difficult time. The boys had been together since they were in diapers. Nick and Brian also lived close by, so the boys went to each other's homes and we all knew they were safe. It's a blessing to have good neighbors. God provided that for me. I was very grateful to have the privilege of raising our family in such a lovely area.

Behind the Scenes…

August bled into September. We muddled through with the three families and no answers. Our marital separation was so incredibly painful week to week. Every morning, I put my feet on the floor and just decided to take care of my kids and get through the next fifteen hours and then sleep and get up and do it all over again the next day.

In October, Craig and I decided to go to our marriage counselor and dissolve our marriage. We made an appointment for October 9 to meet with our counselor, Judy Wilson, in Portland, Maine. I had a Discovery Toys demonstration scheduled that evening in Cape Elizabeth after our appointment. We had tried counseling twice, after the birth of each child, but it didn't help. He wanted out. A lot of water under the bridge. Just too late.

We went to the appointment with Judy. I remember she asked him a question: "Craig, why did you marry Kathy?" His answer was, "Because I knew she would be a good mother to my kids."

That was a huge punch in the gut. Marrying me wasn't about me or who I was. He didn't marry me for me.

Leaving that appointment, I had to head to a demo. I prayed to God it wouldn't be at the home of a Pollyanna in a sweet white apron with the perfect husband and the perfect home with a picket fence and the perfect children with cookies in the oven. God came through. The customer turned out to be a recent divorcee who needed toys for her kids. I enjoyed that group of women so much that night and sold $1,000 worth of toys. That helped so much financially. All the way home, I prayed and thought, "I can do this. I can rise above it and make a new life with the kids." You and me, God. You've got me this far. I trust You can get me the rest of the way.

In the midst of adversity, the concept of vulnerability often feels counterintuitive. Society frequently equates vulnerability with weakness, painting a picture of someone who is exposed and defenseless. However, my journey through hardship, thus far, unveiled a profound truth: vulnerability is, in fact, a source of strength.

That night, Mom and Dad stayed with Josh and Jyl for me. When I got home late after the long drive from Cape

Elizabeth, they had put the kids to bed and gone to bed themselves. There was a note on the counter: "Sleep in in the morning. We will get up with the kids." I thought, "Wow, things are seriously looking up!" I went up and kissed my sleeping babies goodnight and went off to bed with some hope of transition and healing to begin the next day.

The next morning at about eight o'clock, I woke up to my dad pacing around my bed, saying, "Kathy, you've got to get up and come downstairs. Come on now. I've got to talk to you."

I sat up, stunned because my Dad never went in my room. I immediately said, "Dad, where are the kids?"

He said, "Come on. Come downstairs," and he headed down the stairs.

I got up, slowly—and I mean slowly—threw on my dark blue fleece robe, zipped it up, and headed down the stairs to the living room. I was so afraid of what I was going to learn that morning.

Dad was standing there, and my mom wasn't far from him. She started crying and said, "What a way to wake up. . . ."

Dad grabbed my hands with tears running down his face and said, "Kathy, you have had to be so strong for these past months, and I'm really proud of you, but you are going to have to be stronger now than you ever have been."

I stared into his face and said sternly, "Dad, where are my kids?"

He said, "The kids are okay."

Again, I repeated, "Dad, where are my kids?"

He said, "Tammy took them for a walk around the subdivision. They are okay." He continued, "Some people have accused you and Craig of hurting some little kids."

The words went right past my head. Like zero comprehension.

The night before, while Mom and Dad were watching the kids, they received a phone call from a reporter asking for the other side of the story. Mom answered and said he had the wrong number, and he said, "Is this Kathy Belcher's house?" She replied yes. He said, "It's true: Kathy and Craig Belcher have been indicted by a grand jury for felonious sexual assault of two minor children."

She hung up the phone, and they decided to go to bed and deal with whatever this was in the morning. I can't imagine in all my senses what that was like for them that night to lay their heads on their pillows.

I only half-heard my dad's words. I said, "What are you saying to me?" and the phone rang on the kitchen wall. It was Craig.

While driving to the TV shop that morning, he had heard it on the local radio station in his van: "Local couple Craig and Kathy Belcher have been indicted by a grand jury for felonious sexual assault of two minors." Literally, this is how we learned about this horrific nightmare.

He got to work and called the radio station and said, "What the hell is my and my wife's name doing on the radio?" Whoever answered the phone told him it was public information and that he could call the police station for more information. He then called the Conway police station and asked the same question. He asked if he was going to be arrested because he didn't need a scene in front of his business.

The police officer on the other end said, "No, Mr. Belcher, you will not be arrested."

They hung up, and Craig was left completely numb but furious. What was next?

May I just point out here that he didn't even know these children? He had nothing to do with my day care.

The phone rang again. It was Eve, a mom of two kids we had continued watching in the day care after I was shut down. She said, "Kathy, Nick [her husband] just called and said he heard on the radio that you have been indicted. What is going on?" She sounded truly concerned.

I dropped the phone and started screaming, "No, no, no!" I couldn't do this. I didn't even know what this meant. I just knew it wasn't anything good. Would we just get picked up and carted off to jail? I had no idea how the court system worked. I had zero exposure to trials or hearings or what a deposition was, and emotionally, mentally, physically—I was empty. Heck, I had never had a speeding ticket! I was completely devoid of any strength, any energy, any faith, any will.

Imagine yourself for just a minute here. Step into my shoes and picture yourself having gone through these last seven to eight months, and now this. The level of fear. The ridiculousness of the charge. The bearing down of an indescribable albatross. Now . . . get up and feed the baby, hold your little boy. Wonder if your minutes with them are numbered at this time. Smell their hair, look at their little dimpled hands, hear their voices asking for something to eat. Physically shaking while you change your daughter's diaper. Look at the terror in your parents' eyes as they fear what could be coming your way.

This was the Friday of Columbus Day weekend. What were we supposed to do now? Trying to explain what transpired over the course of the next three days is difficult because so much is a blur. I do know that my brother, Tommy, went to work to find us legal representation. There was an attorney in his networking group he met with in Conway once a month. He called him and asked for the best attorney in New Hampshire.

It was then that Mike Dunn entered our lives. He was with a firm called Sheehan, Phinney, Bass and Green, a two-and-a-half-hour drive south in Manchester. Tom called and we made an appointment for Tuesday. It was a long Columbus Day weekend, and it was a grueling wait to get with Mike to know what this was all about.

By the way, the next day, on Saturday, the indictments were in our mailbox. They had been mailed—but completely unsealed. Anyone could have opened them and read them. We faced thirty-three and a half years' imprisonment for felonious sexual assault of two minor children.

I remember that day—Friday—Jylian took her first steps between my dad and brother Tom in the playroom while we all sat in that room just waiting for someone to tell us what to do next. There were quite a few of us at my house all that day.

What was going to happen? The phone was ringing off the wall from newspapers all over the state and region. I'll always remember that. I was scared to death.

Refrain from judgment

To the Editor:

I am shocked about the indictments handed down against Craig and Kathy Belcher, as are all those who know them.

Kathy is an extremely talented and caring child-care provider. As a former educator and a very "Picky" mother, I am extremely particular about any day-care service that we chose for my daughter. Kathy cared for her for two years (encompassing the time period when the alleged offense occurred) and did it with great skill, humor and above all, love. My husband and I believe that charges such as those brought against the Belchers are preposterous.

Also, we believe the charges against Craig are ludicrous. In two years of drop-offs and pick-ups at their house Craig was very rarely home. As everyone who knows Craig and the business he owns is aware, he works from dawn to dusk and beyond, everyday.

These two people are simply incapable of the evil they are allegedly accused of and as of this writing, neither Cathy nor Craig have received official notice, in writing, in person or by phone of the charges brought. Kathy learned of them one week ago by a phone call from a Union Leader reporter. Craig heard the news on radio station WBNC/WMWV.

It would seem decent, fair and it should be the law that people accused of offense of this magnitude be informed before any information is released to the press, just as the names of accident victims are withheld pending notification of next of kin.

Initially, I, like most people, tend to "believe what I read in the papers," if I don't know the people involved. I depend upon the law enforcement and legal systems to have the evidence lined up to "have a case."

In this case we know and believe in the innocence of the alleged perpetrators and now that more than a week has gone by without official notification, my faith in both systems is shattered, as are the Belcher's lives.

They fear that people will believe the accusations, that they may lose both their businesses, their savings and their home in an attempt to pay legal fees to defend themselves. They also fear that whoever is the guilty party or parties may go unpunished, while they may face jail terms if wrongly convicted.

And, the Belchers, being who they are, feel for the child or children involved, hoping that they may recover from their past trauma and from what they will go through at the trial.

We can only guess at the traumatic effects on the Belchers' own children, one aged five years, one 11 months. The ironic thing is that even when acquitted, much of the damage mentioned above cannot be repaired.

Hopefully the people in our community will refrain from passing judgment and will wait for the last-page article announcing an innocent verdict.

In the meantime, a group of friends and supporters have started a Legal Defense Fund for the Belchers to help defray these expenses. Anyone who knows them knows that they are morally incapable of abusing a child.

Contributions may be sent to:

The Belcher Defense Fund
P.O. Box 191
Brownfield, ME 04010

We urge you to give what you can.

Sincerely,
Howard and Margot Miller
South Conway

Carroll County INDEPENDENT

Carroll County Pioneer

The Pioneer labors to remove the underbrush from the Forest of Humanity.

J. J. Burghardt, Publisher — Michelle Gregoire, News Editor

Vol. CVI, No. 42, Est. 1881, Center Ossipee, N.H. 03814, Wed. Oct. 21, 1987

CARROLL COUNTY INDEPENDENT
Wed., October 21, 1987

This was the sweetest thing my brother and others put together to help develop support for us while drowning in false accusation.

1989

NACKEY LOEB

Publisher

lerestimate Governor

ıinks New Hampshire has recent signals from the his effect: we should not d Gregg.
d Gregg does not throw his has a self-effacing manner. shown by recent events.
l the courage to veto the nted to him by the Senate v that would make New haven, should Roe vs. Wade eme Court.

Page 10

To Violate the Law

WASHINGTON (AP) — The jury in Oliver North's Iran-Contra trial was dispatched yesterday to decide the guilt or innocence of the former White House aide with the judge's admonition that no one, including the President, had "the legal authority to order anyone to violate the law."

North has said he had authority from superiors including, he believed, President Reagan, for many of his actions in behalf of the Nicaraguan rebels at a time when official U.S. aid was banned.

Because of the lateness of the hour, jurors were sent to the nearby hotel where they will be sequestered, with orders to begin deliberations today.

U.S. District Judge Gerhard A. Gesell told them "your job is to decide the facts" in the first trial stemming from the mid-1980s affair in which profits from arms sales to Iran were diverted to aid the Nicaraguan rebels.

The judge was specific in his instruction about North's contention that he acted under orders from top White House officials and, he assumed, with Reagan's approval.

"Neither the President nor

NORTH Page 8

County Prosecutor Drops Sexual Assault Charges Against Conway Couple

By PAT GROSSMITH
Union Leader Staff

Charges against a Conway couple accused of conspiring to sexually assault two toddlers were nol prossed yesterday by prosecutors who said the children's mother asked the case be dropped.

Carroll County Attorney William D. Paine II said yesterday the mother felt it was in the best interests of the children if the case were dropped. Now that that has happened, Paine said, Katherine Belcher of Conway and Craig Belcher of Glen "stand as if they were never charged in this matter."

Paine said the children's legal guardian, court-appointed attorney Pamela Albee of Ossipee, agreed with the mother's decision.

The Belchers and their attorneys, at a press conference in Manchester yesterday, maintained they were innocent and the county prosecutor never had any probable cause to charge them in the first place.

"It's just criminal we had to live through this when I was a person who lived by the law and believed that the judicial system protected me and my business with children," said Mrs. Belcher, who now is employed at a motel. She said that the experience has taught her otherwise.

"I trusted that they (prosecutors) did their jobs and they don't," she said.

Mr. Belcher, who owns Mountain Village Television, said the county attorney's announce-

DAYCARE Page 10

›rtion Veto

"The governor feels morally obligated to compel women to complete unintended pregnancies, but his budget proposal contains not one-cent of additional monies for family planning or prenatal care, or WIC (Women Infants and Children) services or child support enforcement," she said. "Now, I ask you, Governor Gregg, what kind of morality is that?" she asked.

On the streets, there were roughly as many citizens in favor of legalized abortions as there were ones who were opposed to it. Those opposed gave their reasons.

Mary Sieve of Windham said, "I wish it were not legal. I think

REACTION Page 10

n burglars doesn't require the ıive alarm system. Good use ʼour belongings better than bells

Page 38

ɔx past Cleveland, 5-2. Page 45

Index

☐ DAILY NUMBER

April 20

The Manchester Union Leader
Friday, April 21, 1989

The state newspaper, Manchester Union Leader, making the announcement that the charges were dropped two years after the nonsense began.

decision, P. 8 | Conway school plans, P. 5

PENDENT

Carroll County Pioneer

814 | Wednesday, October 12, 1988 | 38 Pages In 3 Sections | 40 Cents

)efense lawyers claim evidence ›oints to Belchers' innocence

unty attorney is accused of withholding evidence from the grand jury

arbara Wood Hoyt

SSIPEE — Defense attorneys
raig and Katherine Belcher of
vay have filed motions to dis-
indictments which charge the
e with the sexual assault of a
g girl.

Belchers were indicted a
ago on charges of aggravated
ous sexual assault. They are
ed of conspiring with other,
ntified people, to commit a
l act on a girl younger than 13
y 1984.

girl attended Katherine Bel-
family day-care center at the
er home on East Conway
at the time of the alleged as-
She was enrolled until June
when Belcher closed the center for personal reasons.

The Belchers have pleaded innocent to the charges. Soon after the indictments were announced, a group of citizens, including parents of children who attended Belcher's day-care center, started a support group to help raise legal fees and provide public support for the couple.

Grand jury evidence

The motions filed last week ask the court to dismiss those indictments because Carroll County Attorney William D. Paine II withheld exculpatory evidence from the grand jury.

Exulpatory evidence is evidence which tends to prove a defendant's innocence.

"Despite the availability of exulpatory evidence from physicians and police, the County Attorney failed to present the evidence to the grand jury," wrote Paul W. Hodes of Manchester, Craig Belcher's attorney, in his motion.

"The evidence was important. The evidence was substantial. The evidence was objective and no reasonable trier of fact, having heard such evidence could have found probable cause to indict in this case," Hodes wrote.

Paine denies the attorneys' claims. He said he did not withold any evidence and will file an objection to their motions to dismiss.

"We put in everything we had," Paine said last week. "If I can't convince the grand jury then I'm certainly not going to convince the (trial) jury."

He said he could not comment on the specific information and evidence presented to the grand jury. Defense attorneys are not present during grand jury proceedings and do not have access to the records.

"Because the defendant has no access to the grand jury transcript, she cannot state definitively what information was or was not actually presented by the State to obtain the indictment," wrote W. Michael Dunn of Manchester, Katherine Belcher's attorney, in his motion.

"However, it must be presumed

See COURT - Page A14

This is an example of how front-page news appeared one year after the charges were brought forth. Every time this would happen, the public scrutiny would start all over again for us.

Wed. Jan. 4, 1989

Belchers' lawyers criticize evidence

by Shelly Gregoire

DOVER — Defense lawyers for the Conway couple accused of child sexual abuse had their day in court last Friday.

At a pre-trial hearing in Strafford County Superior Court, Judge Robert H. Temple heard more than two hours of arguments, mostly from the attorneys hired by Craig and Katherine Belcher.

"Judge, this is a prime example of grand jury abuse," said Paul Hodes of the law firm of Hage and Hodes of Manchester, Craig Belcher's lawyer. Kathy Belcher's attorney is W. Michael Dunn of the Manchester law firm of Sheehan, Phinney, Bass and Green. Both are former prosecutors.

At issue were three motions they filed — one to prohibit testimony of the alleged victim and her younger sister, one to make the state turn over the names of grand jury witnesses, and one to dismiss the case so it could not be brought forward again, based on what the grand jury was told or was not told by the prosecutor.

A grand jury in Carroll County in October 1987 indicted the Belchers on charges of aggravated felonious sexual assault of a young girl in May 1984 when the girl was enrolled in Kathy Belcher's home day care program.

Almost 3½ years passed between the time of the alleged assault and the grand jury action. The Belchers had not been arrested and

'Judge, this is a prime example of grand jury abuse.' — Paul Hodes, lawyer for Craig Belcher

Conway police had closed its initial probe of the allegations by the children's mother.

"The indictments in this case came as a shock and a surprise, not only to the defendants but the community up there," said Hodes. Last fall, a defense fund was started by 65 people, who bought newspaper ads to proclaim their support.

Was evidence withheld?

Half of Friday's hearing was held in the judge's chambers, with only the lawyers for the Belchers, Pamela Albee of Ossipee, court-appointed lawyer for the alleged victim and her sister, and William D. Paine II, Carroll County attorney, meeting with the judge.

The Belchers and five other people who appeared to be family or friends waited for more than an hour as the lawyers versed Judge Temple on the details of the case. Temple, who was assigned to the case because he will preside in Carroll County next spring, had not had a chance to look at the extensive files before the hearing.

When the closed meeting was

See BELCHERS - Page 16

The newspaper articles were chronicled by one of my sisters. Reading through the articles many years later puts so many things back into perspective of what transpired over time. It was helpful for writing the book.

Lawyers lambaste prosecutor in Belcher child abuse case

BELCHERS · From Page 1

over, an abbreviated hearing was held in the courtroom, concentrating mostly on Dunn's motion to dismiss the case because he claims Paine manipulated the facts that should have been presented to the grand jury.

Hodes has joined with Dunn in the arguments.

Paine has denied the claim previously and on Friday he told the judge, "I believe, Your Honor, it is my obligation to present a balanced case to the grand jury."

Albee, as the children's guardian, said little at the hearing but in court documents has said the Belchers' lawyers are speculating on what Paine may or may not have done.

(A state grand jury hears evidence only from the prosecutor and witnesses. The accused and their lawyers are not allowed to attend or present evidence.

(It is the duty of the prosecutor to present all evidence available so the grand jury is allowed to make a fair decision on whether the felony probably occurred. If it finds probable cause, it issues an indictment, which allows the case to proceed in criminal court. All proceedings are secret.)

Dunn said Paine, at the time of the indictment, had or should have had evidence which would have caused the grand jury to question Paine's claims, particularly on the identification of the Belchers and lack of physical evidence of sexual abuse.

But Paine, in a telephone interview Friday night, said, "I've got the reports of two psychologists who met with the kids over a period of time and this is what the kids told her." Those reports were entered as evidence in Friday's hearing.

'I believe, Your Honor, it is my obligation to present a balanced case to the grand jury.' — Carroll County Attorney William D. Paine II

May 1, 1984, and they remained there until Belcher closed it in June 1985 for personal reasons.

The mother brought the girls at some time in 1984 to pediatrician Dr. Thomas Packard and psychologist Dr. Edwin Goodall because she was concerned about some behavior problems, said Dunn.

The older girl was then placed in therapy with psychologist Dr. William Nagahiro. When she won a game during a session with Nagahiro April 18, 1985, said Dunn, Nagahiro reached out to touch her when he said congratulations.

The girl jumped up and ran from the room. When the mother entered, worried about her daughter, Nagahiro said, according to Dunn, "I think the girl may have suffered some abuse or trauma. Does she have a babysitter?"

The mother, according to her first entry in a diary she started that day, told her husband that night that Nagahiro had said that perhaps the children had been sexually abused, Dunn said.

The father "turned white and jumped off the couch," said Dunn. When the mother corrected her statement to clarify what Nagahiro had said, the father replied, " 'You know, (the older girl) never liked Kathy Belcher anyway.' "

The following day's diary entry states that the mother told her

to expound at great length on all of these things that happened to her at 13 months old."

"Detective Jones believed the whole thing essentially was contrived and controlled," said Dunn.

Paine said after the hearing that Jones never saw Nagahiro's three-page report and added that there was a personality conflict between Jones and the girls' mother.

Medical records

As to physical evidence, the mother refused to give police permission to obtain medical records. After the indictment, the records were obtained, said Dunn.

Dr. Packard's report in September 1984 indicated he conducted a well-child exam and a genital exam and the child was "fine," said Dunn. Two other visits — one in December 1984 and one in May 1986, a year after the child had left Kathy Belcher's day care — showed the girl was "fine." A doctor in Massachusetts examined her in November 1986. The result: "Fine."

The same was true for the younger girl, said Dunn, who had exams in June 1984, July 1985 and May 1986.

But Dr. Shubin in Baltimore in August 1987 found both girls had been sexually assaulted, said Dunn.

The grand jury had no access to that medical information, he said.

"Essentially what occurred here is the grand jury did not get a fair opportunity to examine the evidence that then existed and so render a fair judgment."

But Paine told the judge the report of psychologist Dr. Donna Harrison stated, "In summary, I find both these children, especially (the older girl), to be credible when explaining in detail the abuse suffered at the hands of Craig and Kathy Belcher.

"In my estimation," Paine said, reading Harrison's report, "these children are among the worst victims of child sexual abuse I have evaluated in my career."

Paine also said Dr. Packard was not specific in answering questions about whether he conducted genital examinations of the girls, adding that the mother said Packard did not.

'Essentially what occurred here is the grand jury did not get a fair opportunity to examine the evidence that then existed and so render a fair judgment.' — W. Michael Dunn, attorney for Kathy Belcher

"I'm absolutely bound by an oath of secrecy on what goes on before the grand jury," said Paine.

The exception is if a judge were to order him to reveal details in a case of "manifest necessity," or life and death. Protecting a defendant's constitutional rights does not qualify, said Paine.

Asked whether he had sufficient evidence at the time he went to the grand jury, Paine said, "I don't try cases I don't think I can win."

One of the psychologists, a Dr. Shubin of Mercy Hospital in Baltimore, is nationally acclaimed for his work in child sexual abuse cases, Paine said.

Identifying the Belchers

But Dunn, Kathy Belcher's lawyer, claims it was the girls' parents who connected the possibility of sexual abuse to the Belchers.

"The fingerpointing was not done by the children first."

The girls were 33 months and 13 months old when first placed in Kathy Belcher's day care around

daughter, "Mommy and Daddy will take care of you...Tell us what bad things Kathy Belcher did to you," said Dunn.

"And that, in my opinion," Dunn said, "is the beginning of the nightmare for the Belcher family."

Nagahiro kept no notes on his counseling sessions with the girl from April until October 1985, said Dunn. "No comments were made by the children for six months."

And the mother's diary was not introduced as evidence to the grand jury, said Dunn.

Two investigators — Brian Collins of the Conway Police Department and Richard Jones of the Carroll County Sheriff's Department — found the statements of the two girls to be confused and contradictory, said Dunn.

Collins testified for five minutes before the grand jury. Jones was not called.

Dunn also complained that the grand jury never heard any reference to the younger girl. "When she was approximately 3½, (the younger girl) suddenly begins

Also, after the indictments, the girls were physically examined by Dr. Lawrence Ricci of the Mid-Maine Medical Center in Waterville. Paine said Dr. Ricci found clear evidence the older girl had been sexually abused.

Paine also said the older girl told her mother on May 14, 1985 that "The babysitter did things to me that were worse than being spanked...She did this to my body and to other children..."

Judge Temple made no decisions on the three motions. He wants a hearing to determine the competency of the girls as witnesses. But he indicated he may act on the motions to order Paine to list the grand jury witnesses and to dismiss the case.

If he issues an order to dismiss before February, the competency hearing will not be held.

If he does not dismiss the case, it may go to trial in late April.

After many, many months of not being able to speak about the abuses of the legal system and the downright egregiousness of this horrible thing happening to us, it was a pressure release to see the attorneys stating the truth while we remained completely silent. It was so, so difficult.

A night on the town with Conway police...page 11

The REPORTER

NORTH CONWAY • NEW HAMPSHIRE • CONWAY

356-5566 THE REPORTER, VOL. 80, NO. 44 WEDNESDAY, NOVEMBER 4, 1987 36 PAGES 3 SECTIONS 30 cents

Conway police deliver

By M. Tracey Ober

The Conway police department is catching more than criminals these days.

Friday morning at 7:35, police officer Laurie Nickerson caught a 6 lb., ½ oz. baby girl when Candice Hutchins, of Fryeburg, Maine, went into labor in front of the police department.

Hutchins was being driven by her mother, Sara Cooper, to Memorial Hospital when she realized they weren't going to make it through Main Street traffic in time. Cooper pulled her Ford Escort into the police parking lot and ran inside.

Nickerson was at the police department doing paperwork when she heard a commotion at the front door.

"I went up and this woman was screaming and pulling me out to the parking lot. I didn't have any time to think," Nickerson said. She went out to the car, where Hutchins was in the last stages of labor. The head had already appeared, so Nickerson just let the rest of the baby slide into her arms. She then cleared the newborn's airway and gave her mouth-to-mouth resuscitation.

Sergeant Chris Canney assisted Nickerson by covering the baby

Funny lady

Belcher case

Indictment basis sought

By M. Tracey Ober

A Conway couple has been charged with a very serious crime. On Oct. 8, a Carroll County Superior Court grand jury handed down an indictment against Katherine Belcher, 30, of Conway and Craig Belcher, 31, of Glen, charging each with two counts of assisting and conspiring with a third person in aggravated felonious sexual assault. If convicted, the two could face a maximum sentence of 7 ½ to 15 years in prison.

Michael Dunn, the lawyer representing Katherine Belcher, said the couple approached him because they were, "absolutely stunned out of their shoes. They are not guilty of any act." As her attorney, Dunn has recommended that all inquiries about the case be referred to him. "I tell you honestly, when she called me and spoke to me, she had no knowledge of the accusations," he said.

The grand jury decided on the basis of presentations by the investigating officers of the Conway Police Department and the county attorney, William D. Paine II, that there was enough evidence to bring the case to trial. Paine could not comment on the witnesses at the secret sessions, but said other witnesses were brought in besides the ones who spurred the investigation.

The 18-month investigation began when a child psychologist suspected a case of child abuse and reported it in December of 1985 to the police department and the Division of Children and Youth Services. According to Paine, the mother of two children who had attended the day care center run by Katherine Belcher, brought them to a child psychologist for treatment. The children were treated sometime after May of 1984 when the events allegedly took place, but before December of 1985 when the case was reported.

"I don't know if they (the Belchers) knew about the investigation, but they were never directly questioned," Paine said,

Indictment on page 2

Another front-page article just weeks after the indictment was handed down to us.

Articles were very lengthy most times. The feeling was like being stripped bare in the town square.

Lawyers criticize prosecutor in child sexual abuse case

COURT - From Page 1

that the only evidence that could have been presented by the State is that which it had in its possession at the time. In the course of discovery, the defense has learned the identity of most witnesses who testified before the grand jury. From this information, the defense has been able to substantially reconstruct those proceedings.

"In order to reach a fair decision on whether to indict the Belchers, the grand jury was entitled to consider all evidence in the hands of the state (or available to it through reasonable effort) that had any bearing on reliability of the medical findings or the indentification of the Belchers as the 'molesters,' " Dunn wrote.

"The State, however, manipulated the evidence in such a way as to deny the grand jury access to this very information, and thus preordained the outcome without regard for fundamental fairness to the defendants," he wrote.

In the motions, defense attorneys say the exculpatory evidence available at the time of the indictments includes a report from the Conway Police Department and of a Carroll County Sheriff's deputy. Conway police looked into the initial report and decided not to prosecute.

Also, the defense attorneys claim that the grand jury did not see reports of a local pediatrician and psychologist who found no evidence of sexual abuse. They cite the prosecutor's failure to interview the Belchers, and the lack of accusations from any other child who attended the day-care center at the same time, despite charges by the victim's parents that another child had also been assaulted.

Although the indictments allege a sexual assault against only one child, the defense attorneys state that further allegations have been made that a younger sister was also involved.

'The State, however,

'We put in everything we had. If I can't convince the grand jury then I'm certainly not going to convince the (trial) jury.' — William D. Paine II, Carroll County attorney, denying defense allegations

sidered that two (of the child's) treating physicians examined her after she left Kathy Belcher's care and neither found any evidence to support Dr. Shubin's findings," Dunn wrote.

Defense attorneys also claim that Paine intentionally excluded the testimony of Deputy Richard Jones, one of the officers who interviewed the children.

Mother's influence questioned

"Deputy Jones, in his deposition testimony, stated that he had, and continues to have, serious doubts regarding the truth of the allegations against the Belchers.

"He believes that the excessive control exerted over the interview by (the children's mother), who objected to the asking of certain questions, coupled with her repeated rehearsal of testimony with the child, tainted the interviews.

"Deputy Jones found the children's testimony so confused and contradictory that it could not be believed. As someone with extensive experience in investigating sexual abuse cases, his opinion was that these children did not understand what they were saying, but rather were repeating a learned story," wrote Dunn.

Dunn claims that the state presented the grand jury with eight pages of the victim's mother's diary, but withheld the remaining pages of the 75-page diary, "an omission that left the grand jurors with the erroneous impression that the Belchers had been identified independently by the children," Dunn wrote.

The mother's influence is questioned in this article. Still the case went on and on.

manipulated the evidence in such a way as to deny the grand jury access to this very information, and thus preordained the outcome without regard for fundamental fairness to the defendants.' — W. Michael Dunn, attorney for Katherine Belcher

Medical records

Dunn claims the only medical information submitted to the grand jury was raw notes by a Dr. Shubin of Baltimore, Md.

"Although it is unclear whether Dr. Shubin appeared before the grand jury to explain those notes, the defense has learned that Dr. Shubin had no knowledge of the children's prior medical history, (his file contained no medical records from other physicians) and thus could not testify as to when any alleged abuse had taken place," wrote Dunn.

"None of the children's regular pediatricians testified despite their availablilty, an omission that resulted in the exclusion of exculpatory medical evidence.

"The grand jury never con-

"The diary entry for April 19, 1986, establishes that it was (the parents), and not (the child) who originally asserted that sexual abuse had, in fact, occurred and that Kathy Belcher was a participant in that abuse. (The mother's) deposition testimony regarding the entry unequivocally corroborates this fact.

"Had this evidence been presented, the grand jurors would have found that the identification of the Belchers was tainted from the start, and refused to issue an indictment."

"The defendant has discovered that October, 1986, the younger sister (then 3½ years old) allegedly began making detailed statements to (psychologist) Dr. Nagahiro concerning sexual abuse that happened when she was 15 months old.

"The fact that so young a child can recount events that allegedly occurred when she was a virtual infant, clearly suggests that the substance of the allegations was learned rather than remembered by that child. When the younger child's statements are considered in light of the mother's diary entries, such a finding becomes more probable than not," Dunn wrote.

A hearing on the motions has been scheduled for Nov. 22. This hearing is the final one before a trial date is scheduled.

More facts are revealed….still the case went on…

Conway Daily Sun

NO.77 CONWAY, N.H. MT. WASHINGTON VALLEY'S DAILY NEWSPAPER 356-2999 FREE

Belcher: 'It's criminal we had to live through this.'

Battle now over, Belchers lash out at criminal justice system

By Adam Hirshan
THE CONWAY DAILY SUN

MANCHESTER — Kathy Belcher and Craig Belcher, charges against them dropped, lashed out yesterday against Carroll County Attorney William Paine and the criminal justice system which has tainted their name.

"I'm not sure there's a word or an expression," Kathy Belcher, of Conway, said when asked how she felt. "It's not really relieved. It's criminal that we had to live through this."

"It's difficult to still have respect for such a farce of a system," Craig Belcher, of Glen, commented.

Paine dropped charges of child sexual assault against the Belchers Tuesday, a year and a half after they were indicted by a grand jury for allegedly abusing a thirteen month old and 2 1/2 year old at Kathy Belcher's day care center in May 1984.

The county attorney said he dropped the case because the mother of the children did not want them to testify at the trial.

Flanked by their attorneys, the Belchers faced the press to give their side of the story.

According to defense counsel, the charges should never have been brought to begin with. The attorneys noted that initial investigations by a Carroll County sheriff and a Conway police detective yielded no evidence of a crime.

see BELCHER page 5

Sparks fly at first SAU meeting

The Conway Daily Sun
Friday, April 1[illegible], 1989

The day after the criminal charges were dropped. Left in ruins financially, and mentally and psychologically scarred for life.

plication for a mining permit on 160 acres that could come within 100 feet of their properties.

The abutters, Gordon and Frances King, Ernest and Constance Boucher, Leonard and Naydene Drew, and Donald and Darlene Burnham, believe they were not given a chance to present their case at an appeal hearing held by the board on Oct. 10, according to Ruth Ham, chairwoman of the Madison Board of Adjustment. None could be reached for comment Tuesday.

After the appeal hearing, the Millham of Laconia, the attorney for Conway Sand and Gravel, but claimed on the hearing record they were not given a chance to rebut the mining company. Donald Burnham stated for the record, "I have other questions that I would like answered and I was not given the chance to ask them nor was anyone else."

Abutters have camps along the shore of Ledge Pond, which is not visible from any highway. The town also owns a portion of the shoreline. The pond is located in

... red with its lawyer last Friday on the question of whether or not to re-open the mining company's appeal at the request of the abutters, Ham said. The abutters are now represented by attorney William Chapman of the Concord law firm of Orr and Reno, which has filed for a rehearing. Millham said Monday he had written to the board opposing a rehearing.

On July 25, the board had denied

See Excavation — Page 12

Malice and neglect are cited in lawsuit against prosecutor

Couple accused in child-abuse case wants to 'set the record straight'

By SHELLY GREGOIRE
Carroll County Independent staff

OSSIPEE — The Conway couple who claim they were falsely accused of child abuse have filed lawsuits against the county attorney and two psychologists for alleged negligence and malicious prosecution.

"My intention is to set the record straight," said Kathy Belcher of Center Conway last week. "It's not

... husband, ...aig Belcher of North Conway, ...ere indicted by a grand jury in ...ctober 1987 on charges of conspiracy and aggravated felonious sexual assault. The indictments claimed that the Belchers and unnamed others sexually molested one of two young girls while the girls, who are sisters, were enrolled at Kathy Belcher's home day-care center in May 1984.

Almost 3½ years passed between the time of the alleged abuse and the grand jury's indictments. The Belchers had not been arrested and Conway police, upon conducting an initial investigation of the claims by the girls' mother, had closed the case for lack of evidence.

However, from August to October of 1987, Carroll County Attorney William D. Paine II presented evidence to a grand jury in Carroll County Superior Court, and after three sessions, the grand jury issued indictments. Paine has said he provided reports from two physicians and the opinions of two psychologists. "The matter was presented to a grand jury and they heard all of the evidence."

The Belchers claimed innocence and each passed two lie-detector tests. Their lawyers claimed that the case never should have been filed, that no evidence of sexual

See Lawsuit — Page 12

OUCH! Madison tax up $10

MADISON — The property tax rate will leap more than $10 this year because revenue did not meet expectations.

Property owners are receiving tax bills that show a rate of $39.98 per $1000 valuation. The rate for 1989 was $29.25.

Town operating expenses went up from $6.33 last year to $11.43 this year, partly because of cost to rebuild two town roads and largely because revenue from building permits plummeted and the selectmen could not hold their annual land auction in 1989. Rebuilding the roads cost more than $3 on the tax rate and the loss of revenue from building permits amounted to more than $2, selectmen said.

The land auction was held up pending resolution of title problems. A small auction was held in 1990.

The school's portion of the property tax rate rose from $21.36 to $26.85. The increase was caused almost entirely by the bond payment for the new addition completed this year.

The county portion of the tax rate increased from $1.56 to $1.70.

CARROLL COUNTY INDEP
Wed., November 7, 1

And eight years of attempting to countersue those responsible begins.

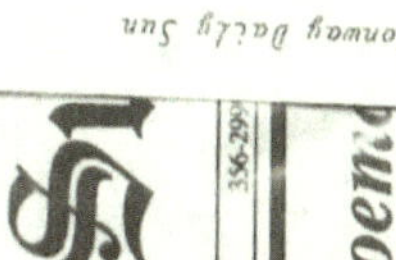

The Conway Daily Su[n]

WEDNESDAY, APRIL 10, 1991 VOL. 3 NO. 67 CONWAY, N.H. MT. WASHINGTON VALLEY'S DAILY NEWSPAPER 356-299[…]

WEDNESDAY

WORLD / NATIONAL

Gorby wants strike ban

MOSCOW (AP) — President Mikhail S. Gorbachev, saying he was trying to avert a national "catastrophe," yesterday proposed a nationwide moratorium on strikes, rallies and demonstrations.

Gorbachev's proposal came as he grappled with growing challenges to his authority. "We face the danger of economic collapse," Gorbachev told the Federation Council, consisting of the leaders of the 15 Soviet republics.

60 soldiers leave Poland

BORNE-SULINOWO, Poland (AP) — A train carried away Soviet missile launchers and 60 soldiers from a formerly top-secret military base yesterday, beginning the Red Army's withdrawal from Poland.

But Polish and Soviet negotiators remained at odds over when the rest of

What about us? ask Parent, Shoem[aker]

Two men complain about how school board appointed Doucette

By John P. Muldoon
THE CONWAY DAILY SUN

CONWAY — Two men who claim they should have been considered as candidates for the vacant seat on the school board are complaining about how the position was filled last week.

Jim Doucette was appointed Thursday to replace Joe Sullivan, who resigned shortly after town elections in March. After Doucette was nominated by board member Theresa Kennett, chairman Gary Poquette had said no one else was interested in the position.

But Dennis Shoemaker and Frank Parent are unhappy with the way the appointment was made.

"I don't feel I got a fair shake at this," says Shoemaker, adding he has no problem with Doucette. "I wish him all the luck in the world. I have no grudge against him."

Parent, who finished last in the three-way race for two seats in this year's election, says he believed he was being formally considered for the third vacancy since Sullivan recommended him when he resigned. "I was a little disappointed that they did not contact me about it," Parent says.

Sullivan notes he called Parent and asked him if he was interested in serving. When Parent said yes, Sullivan says he relayed the information to the school board in his letter of resignation.

see SCHOOL page 6

Belchers' suit against Paine is dismissed

By Adam Hirshan

And as the lawsuit against the prosecutor was dismissed, our hopes sank to ever recover any of what we lost.

Carroll County Pioneer

Vol. CV, No. 41 Established 1881 Center Ossipee, N.H. 03814 Wednesday, October 14, 1987 40 Pages

No place for the homeless

MWV's boom leaves some in the cold

Carroll County Independent

Couple accused of assault at day care

Indictments charge couple with assault of day-care children

The language in this article makes my blood run cold. Indictments…Assault of daycare children…it stirs my very soul that screams of the injustice.

tion Organization.

Prince Saud al-Faisal, the Saudi foreign minister, also responded positively to an Israeli proposal for Mideast peace talks, an official told reporters as Secretary of State James A. Baker III flew here to discuss the peace plan with Syrian President Hafez Assad.

Bush nominee rejected

WASHINGTON (AP) — The Senate Judiciary Committee yesterday rejected President Bush's nomination of Miami judge Kenneth L. Ryskamp to a seat on the 11th U.S. Circuit of Appeals.

Ryskamp is the first of Bush's 77 judicial nominees to be rejected by the Senate and only the fourth in the last decade. Opponents said he was insensitive to civil rights, citing comments from the bench and membership in a country club with a reputation for discriminating against Jews and blacks.

Atlantis touches down

EDWARDS AIR FORCE BASE, Calif. (AP) — Atlantis landed yesterday after an extended mission that featured the first U.S. spacewalk in five years and the deployment of an observatory to study violent mysteries of the universe.

By Scott Andrews
SPECIAL TO THE CONWAY DAILY SUN

CONWAY — The 1991 New Hampshire Professional Cycling Omnium, featuring an international class of 150 top professional cyclists, will premier next month, organizers said yesterday. An official announcement will be made today by Gov. Judd Gregg.

The four days of bicycle races from May 30 to June 2 will extend from the Massachusetts border to the summit of Mount Washington.

The series will start with a 100-mile road race in the Manchester area on Thursday, New Hampshire's celebration of Memorial Day. It will move on to another 100-mile road race Friday in the Lakes Region.

Saturday will feature the high point of the series — literally. A total dis-

see RACE page 6

intendent is asking the judge to stop that secret action from taking place.

Jutras also was tight-lipped yesterday, answering "No comment" to any request for information.

An informed source at Carroll County superior court said the injunction apparently involves "an employment matter."

Jutras has been trying to leave SAU 9. Last year he applied for jobs in New York and Connecticut.

Belchers may appeal to supreme court

By John P. Mudoon
THE CONWAY DAILY SUN

OSSIPEE — Despite the superior court's ruling that county attorney Bill Paine is immune from liability in pursuing his professional duties, Craig and Kathy Belcher are asking judge Bruce Mohl to reconsider his "summary judgment," and their lawyers are threatening to bring the case to the state supreme court.

Mohl issued the judgment saying, "To permit parties…to second guess a prosecutor's decison to take a case to the grand jury in the context of imposing personal liability of the prosecutor, carries a substantial risk that a prosecutor…will not be able to do his job effectively, diligently and without fear of being sued."

In appealing Mohl's summary judgment declaring Paine immune, the Belchers say they are not suing Paine in his role as prosecutor but rather as investigator in a child abuse case brought against them in 1987.

Craig and Kathy Belcher, both of Conway, were indicted on Oct. 8, 1987, for alleged felonious sexual assault of a girl who was then three years old. The case, however, was

see BELCHERS page 8

57 years ago wind gusted to 231 mph

MOUNT WASHINGTON (AP) — Winds gusted to 113 mph on Mount Washington on Thursday, temperatures hovered at 12 degrees and the wind chill was 50-below zero.

"It's nothing unusual," said Ken Rancourt, a meteorologist who spends every other week in the Mount Washington Observatory.

see WIND page 10

CHILDREN'S PARADE

4th annual children's parade, 10 a.m., today, North Conway Village.

We had appeals to the Superior Court and to the Supreme Court.

THE CARROLL COUNTY INDEPE

Wednesday, October 28, 19

NOTICE

County INDEPENDENT

Carroll County Pioneer

Vol. CVI, No. 43 | Established 1851 | Center Ossipee, N.H. 03814 | Wednesday, October 28, 1987 | 52 Pages

Defense fund started by Belchers' supporters

by Barbara Wood Hoyt

CONWAY — A group of people have signed and are circulating a petition to show their support for a Conway couple who were indicted two weeks ago in a sexual assault case.

Craig and Kathy Belcher both pleaded innocent to the charges at a hearing last week.

More than 65 people have signed a notice which states that they know the Belchers and believe they are innocent. A fund has been created to help the Belchers pay for legal fees.

They have published the notice, including all the signatures, in a newspaper advertisement this week to help get their point across.

In an interview Saturday, Kathy's brother, Tom Cormier, and the mothers of three children who attend Kathy's day-care program said the media and legal system have treated the couple unfairly.

They said they are concerned because they believe many people read of an indictment and assume guilt. "How many people even know what the word indicted means?" said Eve Teixeira of Intervale.

An indictment by a grand jury is a formal written accusation, drawn up and submitted under oath by the prosecuting attorney. The grand jury must determine whether the accusation, if proved, is sufficient for a conviction. The grand jury does not hear defense arguments; an indictment simply places the matter before superior court, and a trial may be held.

At the earliest, a trial will not be set in the Belcher case until next April. In the meantime, these supporters said, the Belchers' lives have been devastated.

Development alone won't the costs of Conway's gro

by Martha Carlson

News analysis

CONWAY — How much does development cost? The taxpayers of Conway, its school system and its eight village precincts are about to find out.

Taxes are up this year. Conway voters can expect to spend nearly $29 million in the next five years for major capital projects. Despite a 67 percent increase in the town's tax base, it appears new growth alone cannot finance those costs.

The New Hampshire Department of Revenue Administration set Conway's tax rate last week at 6 percent above the 1986 rate. School district taxes jumped 10 percent. Conway Village's rate climbed 12 percent. Townwide municipal costs dropped 1 percent. Combined with a larger tax base, the town budget reduction balanced the school increase to give most Conway precincts only a 6 or 7 percent tax hike.

Higher tax bills this year are only the beginning. This year the voters approved a record $16,251,900 in capital projects. In the next five years, other town projects, a new landfill or incinerator and a new elementary school could boost the capital budget to $29 million. None of these costs will begin to reflect on tax bills until 1988.

"Add it up," Conway's assistant town manager John Walsh said recently. "One of the reasons the town is looking at some very heavy costs is the infrastructure hasn't been put in place to keep up with all the growth."

For the past decade, while it experienced one of the fastest growth rates in New Hampshire, Conway has avoided spending money on the structural equipment that makes towns work — new schools, roads and pipes — its infrastructure of permanent facilities. Conway has not floated a bond issue since 1974 when taxpayers spent $425,000 to build a bridge. The last major school project was Kennett High's expansion in 1980.

Conway Village is the only neighborhood to have invested in a full array of town services: water, sewer, fire and lights. North Conway, with a modern water syste residents, w water servic facilities un

"The tow reluctant to or to save town mana represent in planning by has grown wanted to be

Concerned tion of Con voters were attitude this $12 million system and system for allocated m for expansi water syster

The vote $600,000 tow road equipr tage lagoon be upgrade Conway Vil way for ano

(Contin

• Taxes

Historical Society wants create $2.5m art museu

The defense fund that was created to help us fight the wave of injustice was a really beautiful beacon of hope in a dark time.

Charges dropped against Belchers

Belchers want to clear their names

By Jim Graham

Now that charges of sexual abuse of two children have been dropped against them, Katherine and Craig Belcher are struggling to salvage what is left of their reputations in the small, closely knit communities of the Mount Washington Valley they call home.

In October 1987, the Belchers were indicted by a Carroll County grand jury on charges of conspiring to sexually assault two minors who attended their day care center in East Conway. The children were 13 months and 2 ½ years old at the time the alleged abuse took place.

Carroll County Attorney William D. Paine II dropped those charges April 19 when the mother and a psychologist who had examined the children both agreed that it was in the best interests of the children not to proceed with the case.

"People will never know the impact this has had on my family."

— Katherine Belcher

THIS WAS IN RED INK

Following the April 19 action, Paine said in a prepared statement that the Belchers "stand as if they were never charged in this matter."

But that may not be enough for the Belchers, who withstood intense public scrutiny and personal turmoil for 18 months after the indictments were brought.

"People will never know the impact this has had on my family," Katherine Belcher said.

At a press conference with their defense counsel in Manchester on Thursday, both Katherine Belcher,

Belchers on page 4

An 18-month ordeal ended for Katherine and Craig Belcher last week when charges of sexual assault of two young children were dropped by Carroll County District Attorney William D. Paine II. Celebrating the victory are, left to right, Michael Dunn, defense attorney; Katherine Belcher; Sara Crosby, defense attorney; Craig Belcher; and Pual Hodes, defense attorney.

Jim Graham photo

The Reporter 4/26/89

cont'd from page 1

31, and Craig, 32, showed some of the bitterness the case has left them.

"It's criminal that we had to live through this for 18 months," said a teary eyed Katherine Belcher, "when I was a person who lived by the law and believed in the law and the judicial system that protected me and my business with children...and it doesn't continue to do that in my mind.

"I trusted that they (prosecutors) did their job and they didn't."

The Belchers, who are separated, both felt the effects of the case on their businesses. Katherine Belcher now works at a local hotel and no longer runs a child care business. Craig Belcher, who own Mountain Village Television, said his business has only begun to recoup a 60 percent drop in sales after the charges were first made public.

The Belchers' defense attorneys refused to comment on whether they are considering filing counter charges against the state or the mother involved.

But in a prepared statement, the Belchers' attorneys charged that Paine "failed to do a complete investigation of the case before seeking indictments, a failure which resulted in insufficient, incomplete and misleading information being presented to the grand jury."

Katherine Belcher is represented by attorneys W. Michael Dunn and Sara Crosby of Sheehan, Phinney, Bass and Green of Manchester, and Craig Belcher is represented by Paul Hodes of Hage and Hodes of Manchester.

The two investigating officers, Detective Brian Collins of the Conway Police Department and Deputy Richard Jones of the Carroll County Sheriff's Office, both testified in pretrial actions that they believed there was no probable cause to charge the Belchers with sexual abuse.

"Deputy Jones interviewed the alleged victims on two occasions and testified that he had and continues to have serious doubts regarding the truth of the allegations against the Belchers," the defense team's statement read. "He found that the children's testimony was so confused and contradictory that it could not be believed."

Detective Collins also interviewed the children and testified that he closed the filed on May 198[illegible] with the notation, "Unfounded."

THE REPORTER

April 26, 1989

Here we are. I'm not sure what page but it was printed on my birthday. I turned 32 this day. This is Craig and I posing with all three attorneys who defended us. Criminal charges were dropped on the 19th.

10.77 CONWAY, N.H. MT. WASHINGTON VALLEY'S DAILY NEWSPAPER 356-2999 FRI

Belcher: 'It's criminal we had to live through this.'

Battle now over, Belchers lash out at criminal justice system

By Adam Hirshan
THE CONWAY DAILY SUN

MANCHESTER — Kathy Belcher and Craig Belcher, charges against them dropped, lashed out yesterday against Carroll County Attorney William Paine and the criminal justice system which has tainted their name.

"I'm not sure there's a word or an expression," Kathy Belcher, of Conway, said when asked how she felt. "It's not really relieved. It's criminal that we had to live through this."

"It's difficult to still have respect for such a farce of a system," Craig Belcher, of Glen, commented.

Paine dropped charges of child sexual assault against the Belchers Tuesday, a year and a half after they were indicted by a grand jury for allegedly abusing a thirteen month old and 2 1/2 year old at Kathy Belcher's day care center in May 1984.

The county attorney said he dropped the case because the mother of the children did not want them to testify at the trial.

Flanked by their attorneys, the Belchers faced the press to give their side of the story.

According to defense counsel, the charges should never have been brought to begin with. The attorneys noted that initial investigation by a Carroll County sheriff and Conway police detective yielded no evidence of a crime.

see BELCHER page

THE CONWAY DAILY SUN, Friday, April 21, 1989—Page 5

BELCHER *from page one*

by a Carroll County sheriff and a Conway police detective yielded no evidence of a crime.

"Deputy Jones interviewed the alleged victims on two occasions and testified that he had and continues to have serious doubts regarding the truth of the allegations against the Belchers. He found the children's testimony was so confused and contradictory that it could not be believed.

"Detective Collins also interviewed the children and testified at his deposition that he closed the file in May of 1987 with a notation: 'Unfounded,' and conducted no further investigation of the case," stated a press released issued by the Belchers' attorneys.

The lawyers point out that if the children were ever sexually assaulted, as some medical evidence indicates, the abuse did not take place at the Belchers' day care center or by the Belchers.

"A Conway area pediatrician, experienced in recognizing sexually abused children, testified in his deposition that he gave the alleged victims complete physical examinations both during and after they left Kathy Belcher's day care center and that he found no evidence to suggest abuse," the attorneys stated.

According to the attorneys, the expert testimony of two psychologists that apparently convinced the grand jury to hand down indictments did not take into account the parents' role in identifying the Belchers.

"Lengthy diary entries and the parents' deposition testimony established that the parents initially identified the Belchers as the alleged abusers despite the fact that numerous other adults, including personnel from other day care centers, had access to the children after they left the Belchers' care in June of then subjected to repeated and suggestive interviews, a process that defense counsel believes irreversibly tainted the identification of the Belchers."

The Belchers are especially bitter about the way they had been notified of the grand jury indictments. Both said they had never been interviewed by police or given a chance to respond to the allegations.

Kathy Belcher was told of the indictment by her father, who had been notified by someone who learned of it in a newspaper report. "He was pacing my room and crying. I thought someone had died — like one of my children. People will never know the impact this has had on my family."

"I walked into my business that morning," explained Craig Belcher, proprietor of Mountain Village TV. "The phone rang and a friend asked if I heard the news on the local radio station. I immediately went into total shock. I just wanted to hide my head ion my coat."

Craig Belcher said his business immediately dropped off by 60 percent. Kathy Belcher was forced to leave her chosen occupation involving children and take a job at a motel.

Yet both stayed in the community and, with the support of friends and relatives, prepared their defense.

"What else could I do but fight?," asked Craig Belcher. "And that's what we've been doing for a year and a half."

The battle has been costly.

"This defense broke our clients financially, utterly broke them,"

said Crai
month, Jud
make the
attorneys w

The Belch
price.

Conway Daily Sun
Friday, April 21, 1989

The articles written after the charges were dropped were still riddled with inaccuracies. It's the nature of the beast, unfortunately.

All aboard! Trains run Saturday, P. A6

Carroll County INDEP

Vol. CVIII, No. 17 Established 1881 Center Ossipee, N.H. 03814

Belchers declare their innocence

Sexual-abuse case dropped after mother refuses to let children testify

by Shelly Gregoire

MANCHESTER — To proclaim the innocence of their clients, lawyers for Craig and Kathy Belcher held a press conference here last Thursday.

Kathy Belcher, 31, of Conway and Craig Belcher, 32, of Glen were indicted by a grand jury in Carroll County Superior Court in October 1987 for allegedly conspiring with another, unknown person to sexually abuse a young girl in May 1984. The prosecution claimed the abuse occurred whil-

Last Tuesday, just before Dr. Dennis Harrison, a Baltimore psychologist, was to answer questions under oath, Harrison and the children's mother asked Carroll County Attorney William D. Paine II to drop the charges against the Belchers.

Paine complied and the case cannot be brought against the Belchers again.

'This case was not dropped because of any technical problems the state had. There was no case.' — W. Michael Dunn, attorney for Kathy Belcher

"I have never before ...

.les, which the mother reportedly had release at that time.

...nd Hodes said they told Paine several 'ou can't go forward with what you've

...said Saturday that he had in his investiga- a report from a physician who had ex- ...he girls that year and a letter from their doctor, as well as the reports of two ...gists.

...'s physical evidence of sexual abuse. The said that the Belchers did it," he said.

...only thing I would have done differently is had more investigation time from someone I more time to pursue it," said Paine.

...he added. "Twenty-three grand jurors out ...t on this case," and heard evidence at three ... The standard used, he said, is the question: ...obable that a crime occurred."

tell the judge what ... the Belchers in the ... remember." The girl ... of the alleged crime.

"She had a lot ... been real and might ...

It is Albee's con... story. It was so mech... voice was different ...

Hodes, in the pres... both trained inves... children's comments ... tradictory that they c...

Psychologist's rol...

After the police in... was referred by an ... Baltimore, "a psycho...

CARROLL COUNTY INDEPENDENT
Wed. April 26, 1989

This was the regional paper. We weren't protected anywhere in the state and even beyond.

Chapter Five

Silhouettes of Doubt

My meeting with Mike on Tuesday and one of his law partners, Sara Crosby, gave us more clarity. I remember the long ride to their office and the millions of thoughts and fears scrolling over and over in my head. I was physically ill. I must have left the kids with my parents or my sister; I don't recall. I just know they weren't in the room with us there. The day was gray outside, and our appointment was at two o'clock.

Mike was about ten years older than me. He was heavyset, had gray, wiry hair, and noticeably had a prosthesis for one of his eyes. He was a burly Irishman yet had a sweet side to him that was both curious and intentional about getting to know who Craig and I were. He sat across from me at their conference room table. He wore a white button-down shirt with his tie loosened and dark suit pants. Sara, who worked with him on his cases and was also a fully licensed attorney, sat in on the meeting as well. She was tall and very slender and dressed professionally with short, dark hair. They both had a long, yellow legal pad in front of them.

I could tell our story was very disturbing to Sara as she asked her questions. As I answered, it was quite evident that she was wanting many more answers from the prosecutor who had brought this case to the grand jury. Sara let Mike lead the questioning, and he explained the charges we were facing. There was much to sort out. We then learned who the accusers were and what they were accusing us of doing.

The backstory we learned that day is that for an entire year before this all came down, the Conway Police Department had investigated a claim made by the parents that we had, allegedly, sexually abused their children. For obvious reasons to protect the identity of the children, I will call them A and B. When you learn how this whole thing was fabricated, you will never believe how this could possibly have ended up in our living room—ever.

Without our knowledge, the police interviewed several families who were part of the day care the first time I was in business, including Sally and Ned Baldwin, Sam's parents, and Howard and Margo Miller, Jessica's parents, both of whom told the police nothing happened to their children. They allowed Jessica and Sam to be questioned. The police met with A and B multiple times, carefully interviewing them. The police report explains what was asked of them and how they responded. They asked the girls if there were other children who had the same things happen to them, and A said, "Yes, Sam and Jessica." It was determined by the police detectives that the mother coached them each time prior to the interviews, and the police could tell by these little girls' answers that was the case. After a year of interviewing the other parents and children and investigations of allegations, the police detectives closed the case and marked the claim unfounded.

Strangely—a little side note here—unbeknownst to me, I actually did a Discovery Toys demo at the home of one of the detectives on the case, Brian Collins, during that time frame. I later learned he was an advocate for us throughout the time prior to indictment and also when the charges were brought. He told the prosecutor not to bother asking him to testify on behalf of the state because he would testify on our behalf that the accusations were unfounded. I remember later learning about him being so upset that Attorney Paine, the county prosecutor, pursued the indictment after Brian and the police department had, in his opinion, done a thorough job and closed the file.

The mother pushed and pushed the prosecutor to continue to bring it before the grand jury. The first time, it was denied. Then the mother hired a "forensic psychologist," Dennis Harrison, who she saw on *The Phil Donahue Show* to come and speak with her kids and do a video with each of them. He charged $1,000 an hour to create these bogus videos to convince a grand jury. The girls never said a single word on the videos. He asked them all leading questions, and the girls didn't answer—they just made gestures with their hands to represent yes and no and "I don't know." Keep in mind, these girls were three years old and eighteen months old when the abuse allegedly occurred. This guy was asking a three-year-old to remember something that allegedly happened when she was eighteen months old. They were now about five and three. These videos were presented to the grand jury, the grand jury denied the first time in September, so it was presented a second time in October of that year and we were indicted. There will be much to learn about the imposter Dennis Harrison.

Trial was set for April 1988.

My parents moved in with me for two weeks when the charges were revealed. They were scared for my safety and that of Josh and Jylian. Though we were innocent of these charges, Dad knew people could be crazy in believing everything they read in the newspapers or heard on the radio.

My child care was closed, and I had no job again. Not a soul came through the door of the TV shop for three weeks. Craig eventually had to sell the business to his employee, Larry. At one point, Craig told me he sat with a revolver in his lap several times over the course of those eighteen months that followed. Josh was the only reason he didn't take his life. This was just awful for him. I feared that he would take his life every day. Josh would have been ruined if that had happened. He worshiped his daddy.

Over time, I lost my Discovery Toys business. I had grown that business to sixty-eight people selling beneath me in a multilevel marketing construct, and I loved it. Several good friends scheduled demos for me for the fall after the charges happened. Some rooms were full of guests, but I came to learn that they were coming only to lay eyes on me or to try to get the story and juicy details. I was instructed to not discuss the case with anyone—anywhere. I was silenced month after month. It was brutal to not be able to tell the whole story—the real facts—and how this really came about. How it didn't belong in either of our lives. Many of the people didn't buy toys. But I persevered. I had to.

The last time I scheduled an in-home demonstration, I had to drive over an hour out of town to do a demo with the hope that people would still allow me to come and teach. I needed to be far enough away that it was likely that no one would know about my charges—everything would be splashed all over the front page of newspapers every time there was a pretrial conference, hearing, or deposition. We were in the state papers and even *The Boston Globe*. It was going to be difficult to go any distance to try to get away from it.

One night, a whole year after the charges were brought against us, I was really needing the income from this season of selling. I had been traveling well over an hour to do this demo. This particular demo was for a mom of four kids in November 1988. Those demos were important because people were shopping for Christmas, and the hostess would really get some great benefits in the form of free toys and games for hosting. I was completely exhausted, so Mom asked to come with me in case I couldn't drive home.

This hostess, Mary, was in dire need of Christmas presents for her kids, so I worked her pretty hard prior to the demo by collecting outside orders from those who couldn't attend, and she worked diligently to get her guest list to be there. It always worked out better for her if they attended in person. She was connected to a school and child care, and right up until that afternoon, she had twenty-eight teachers and faculty confirmed to be there. It was going to be awesome! My prayer was that she would qualify for $1,000 in free products.

Mom and I arrived forty-five minutes before party time to get set up and see how I could help Mary get ready. Mom waited in the car, and I went up to the door and knocked. When Mary answered, she had the saddest face. I said, "Are you ready to do this?"

She said, "No one is coming."

Evidently, around five o'clock that afternoon, one of her guests called her and asked who was doing the demo. Mary told her my name. The person said, "I won't be coming or buying, and I'm sorry for you. I have no interest in supporting the business of a sexual abuser." The call ended, and evidently that friend contacted all the rest.

I was completely stunned. This was a year later and over an hour away from my home. The charges against us had followed me and haunted me over and over and over. Mary told me she had used her last $45 to buy food for the demonstration. And of course, she was missing out on the hostess benefit of free toys for her kids Christmas morning. I had nothing to give her because I was in the same set of financial circumstances. I needed that demo to feed my kids, too.

I walked back to the car, put my crate of toys in the back, and got in the driver's seat. I couldn't even speak. Mom asked what had happened. I started to drive, and I couldn't talk—literally. She got very quiet, and we drove for probably twenty minutes before I could tell her what was said at the door. She started to cry, and I felt so badly that she, too, was carrying the burden of this pain. I couldn't cry—I was out of tears. I just didn't talk the whole way home.

Voices in the Storm…

Over the course of the next eighteen months, both Craig and I took polygraphs conducted by the state police. They were delivered to the desk of the prosecutor, and even though we passed them, it still made no difference. Now, this will come out as a complete mental and emotional dump, but it is about the only way I can do it. So much time was involved in this case, and so many things took place, but these are some of the things we uncovered in discovery. Our attorneys worked so hard on this case. Michael's firm and Craig's attorney, Paul Hodes, represented us in both the criminal case and then when we turned around and sued the psychologists who accused us—not the family who accused us but the two psychologists—and attempted to sue the prosecutor who was grossly irresponsible, reckless, and negligent. During the criminal side of this story, the following happened.

April 19, 1986: This is How it All Began…

Prior to the charges being brought, the mother had taken A and B to a local psychologist, William Nagahiro, because they were afraid of the loud noise from hot air balloons and vacuum cleaners. The girls were three and eighteen months,

I think, at this time. Do you know any child who would be startled by the loud noise of the burner in a hot air balloon or maybe how loud a vacuum might be? Ya, me too.

One day while at therapy, Nagahiro was playing the game of Trouble with A. He was in his office alone with her, and the mother was in the waiting room. This is all documented, by the way, from his deposition. "A" won the game of Trouble, and he leaned over to touch her on the arm and said, "Good job." She jumped up and ran out of the room. The mother came to the door and asked him what he had done to her. He explained what had happened. He said to the mother, "I think something has happened to A, and does she have a sitter?" (He did not say anything about sexual abuse to the mother at that time.) Why on earth would he ask that question—"Does she have a babysitter?"—out of nowhere? This is still a mystery to me. Usually, if a professional suspects any abuse, they consider all people in the child's life suspects until proven otherwise, including parents and family members.

According to the mother's diary, and confirmed at her deposition, when she went home she said to the girl's father, who was lying on the sofa, "Dr. Nagahiro thinks the girls have been sexually abused."

The father jumped off the sofa and said, "What are you saying?"

In the mother's diary, she writes that they then discussed all the babysitters the girls had had. I had not had them in my care at this point for almost two years. They had been with another child care for all that time. The mother said that A never liked taking a nap at Kathy Belcher's house. According to the same diary, the next day, when the girls woke up and A came into the bathroom, the mother picked her up and told her that if Kathy Belcher had done anything to her, she was going to take care of it. She then said that A cried and said she didn't like to take naps there. I don't know any three-year-old who loves to take a nap even if they need it. My name was pulled out of a hat containing all the babysitters these girls had had.

The mother took this interaction to Nagahiro, and he proceeded to take it to the authorities and the fabrication began. And that is how this whole thing started. I believe the prosecutor was coaching the mother on how to make the case stick to the grand jury. Attorney Paine had presented it to the grand jury in September, and it was denied. Then the mother hired "Dr." Harrison, whom she saw on *The Phil Donahue Show* professing to be a forensic psychologist. A forensic psychologist is a professional who applies principles of psychology to the legal and criminal justice systems. They often work in various capacities, including assessing individuals involved in legal cases, providing expert testimony in court, and consulting with law enforcement on criminal behavior and profiling.

Forensic psychologists may conduct psychological evaluations of defendants to determine their competency to stand trial, assess mental state at the time of an offense, or provide insights into a person's psychological profile. They also engage in research related to criminal behavior, help with jury selection, and may offer therapy to victims or offenders. Their work blends both psychological expertise and an understanding of legal principles to aid in the administration of justice.

Harrison traveled to North Conway to conduct a video interview with each of the girls for $1,000 per hour. In 1987, that was pretty good money, wasn't it? He then would testify before the grand jury if necessary, but in our case, the videos were what was presented. We had an opportunity to view the interviews with the girls. As he sat with A, he asked leading questions. He asked her a question about what Craig or I had done to her, and she made hand signals like pointing her hand up for yes and down for no, and in the middle if she didn't know.

Then it became a game to her, and he wasn't getting any clear answer to his questions, so he said, "You don't want to talk about the bad things Craig and Kathy did to you, do you?" She never in the whole interview said a word about anything we had done to her or her sister. The video with B was very short, as I remember it, because she was about eighteen months old when the alleged abuse occurred, and asking her at three years old what she remembered at age eighteen months was absurd. Still, it sickens me that the content of that video, along with the full investigation by the police detectives, was not enough for this to all go away long before it ever rang my telephone. It still went forward to trial.

Later in the case, the parents divorced, and our attorneys discovered the mother and Harrison were having an affair. She uprooted the girls and moved to Columbia, Maryland, where she pursued that relationship.

Then came the real shocker: Harrison was not a forensic psychologist. He had his PhD in education. Over sixty complaints had been placed against him at the Maryland board.

My attorneys discovered he was connected to and seen as the kingpin of the so-called "underground railroad." In this organization, parents whose kids had allegedly been victimized by the other parent would turn their children over to complete strangers, who would change the color of the kids' hair and change their names and pass them from city to town across the country so the accused parent could not find them.

Thankfully, the girls in our case were not subjected to this, but Harrison was found to be the jackass over this enterprise. He would manipulate these parents, who suspected their spouse—whom they were divorcing in most cases—of abuse, to allow him to do this to their children and be compensated for it. Complete strangers all around the country; little kids not knowing where they were or who they were with.

Once these parents hired Harrison, he would then have the parents bring their child or children to a pediatric gynecologist, Dr. Sabin, who practiced at Johns Hopkins University Center in Maryland. Sabin would examine the girls and devise a report with a diagram on a standardized document describing where the presumed vaginal damage was, and so on. We uncovered that Harrison and Sabin had twenty-three other cases going on around the country at the same time. They didn't care that their flagrant negligence was destroying families; they were compensated for it. My attorneys pulled all that together. Each of the cases had the same report, with an identical diagram of purported vaginal damage.

As the case against us dragged on, I was dying in spirit and emotion. When the day was done and all was still, I found myself devoid of feeling. It was as though my hands were tied behind my back and there wasn't a living soul who could understand what I was feeling or going through. The social abuse I experienced was so intense, and every time I turned around, the newspapers were broadcasting fake news, a total misrepresentation of facts like I had never seen. That was me they were talking about. It just had to be someone else's story—not mine. And still, I couldn't say a word—to the press or anyone else, for that matter.

My life was constantly tossed back and forth between emotions: trying to heal from separation, divorce, and rejection, and then this tsunami of false allegations and the terror of the thought of not seeing my children grow up. Was I going to be one of "those people" who are innocent but go to jail? That played over and over in my mind, day after day after day. Where was God with all these answers? When would He squelch the excruciating anxiety of not knowing? That little voice on my shoulder would whisper in my ear, "He's not here. He's not real. He left you all alone to figure all this out."

In her diary, the mother of the alleged victims accused Craig of taking photos of the girls. She accused me of mutilating rabbits in my basement and threatening the children that if they told anyone what we were doing to them, what was happening to the rabbits would happen to them. A and B never uttered a word about that.

Interestingly, the allegations were identical to newspaper descriptions of those in the significant McMartin day-care case happening in California at the same time. The mother in our case was adamant about the same thing happening at my home. Later, she told the prosecutor she didn't think the allegations describing the rabbits in the basement were true after all. Even after this fiasco, the case still went on.

The mother's diary stated that every morning before the girls could have breakfast, they had to tell her one bad thing that Craig and Kathy Belcher had done to them. Then they could have their food. Still the case went on.

When the girls were going to be interviewed by the police, the mother asked the police what kinds of things they intended to ask. She was screening and controlling the questions the whole time. That was according to the deposition of the detective that occurred later in the case. The police detective told her that A (B was still a baby) would draw a picture of a penis since the mother was saying that Craig was involved with them physically. This was a setup to see if the mother would coach them. Indeed, the next day when they had the interview, A drew quite an accurate likeness. Someone had taught her how to draw it. This you can find in the deposition of Brian Collins, I believe. The case still went forward, even when the police had this kind of evidence and closed the case three months before the prosecutor went before the grand jury.

Local pediatrician Dr. Tom Packard was the girls' physician. He did all their wellness checks and never found any evidence of abuse—either kind—in them. He was deposed and testified to this. Dr. Packard was the state physician for the State of New Hampshire at one time and the pediatrician for my children and for many of the children in my day care. He was very familiar with my child-care center.

There are no words to describe how I felt when I learned that my local police department had been investigating Craig and me for an entire year before these charges were brought forward. They interviewed some of the parents who were good friends of mine. Imagine the first phone call from the authorities—what would you think? I had known these folks for four years by that time. Josh and their children were friends; we spent birthday parties and playdates together—and by the way, they were asked not to say anything to me, obviously, because neither of them did. For me, it was the most exposing, embarrassing, violating feeling that I can describe. I was completely innocent and yet felt so accused. Have you ever been in a situation like that? Falsely accused of something, and your voice is silenced and your hands are tied behind your back? My faith was being tested to a breaking point. I was so full of despair.

Chapter Six

And the Band Stops Playing…

I believe it was sometime in the late summer of 1988 that my attorneys traveled to Columbia, Maryland, to find out all they could about Harrison. They found out from the police department that Harrison had made a public claim that someone had fired shots into his home. It is alleged that he did this to raise attention for himself to gain notoriety. The police found that he fired the shots himself with his own gun. Still the case went on.

Two years later to the day (April 19) that Nagahiro made the first accusation to the Conway Police Department, Harrison was scheduled to appear at Sheehan, Phinney, Bass, and Greene in Manchester for his deposition. My attorneys had all the goods on him, and they were ready. They just needed him under oath. I went that day to sit in on that long-awaited deposition. My brother, Tom, came with me. Harrison asked the mother to come with the girls. They were two floors down in the office building.

When Harrison came into the room, I wanted to vomit. There he was with his Italian-stallion look, with his gold chain around his neck, his dark wavy hair, and his navy sport coat. He sat himself down for about what felt like ten minutes. He then proceeded to get up from the table, refused to go under oath, and walked out of the room with his new attorney in tow. He went down to the lobby and asked the mother to come meet him.

They stood across the street arguing in front of Dunkin' Donuts. Mike asked his assistant to get him a subpoena quickly. Then he went downstairs, went across the street, put the subpoena in Harrison's pocket, and said, "Consider yourself served." Harrison said, "Why don't you get some class?" Mike said, "I'll see you upstairs." Harrison never returned to the room.

After eighteen months of the most egregious proceedings and grueling abuse of justice, Harrison, that same day, convinced the mother to drop the charges against us. He told her that our attorneys had the goods on him and that they were going to ruin everything he had in place. Like he was some kind of hero for children. The mother did as he asked—remember this was what this woman lived and breathed every day for two years. She told the prosecutor to drop the charges, and it was over.

Bill Paine, the prosecutor, came into the conference room and made an announcement that the mother was dropping the charges. We all sat there in silence for what felt like twenty minutes. The moment the words "drop the charges" echoed in that conference room, time seemed to stand still. It was as if the air had thickened, wrapping around me, and for a fleeting instant, I struggled to comprehend the significance of what had just transpired. The tension that had clung to my shoulders for over a year suddenly began to dissipate, replaced by a surge of emotions I had long kept bottled up.

We were stunned—all of us except Bill Paine. He asked if anyone was up for going to lunch, all friendly-like and acting like it was just another day at the office. I had some serious forgiveness work to do around knowing that man. A prosecutor he wasn't.

When Josh turned four and Jyl was still a baby, probably around December 1986, I had been seeking a church environment for them to learn about God and Jesus. I was raised a Catholic from the cradle. I attended parochial school until grade seven, then went into the public school system until graduation. Every Sunday when I was a kid, my family was at church lined up in the pew, sitting still and not making a move unless you wanted the proverbial "look" from Mom. I promise you, you didn't want that!

I was described as a good little Catholic girl. I wouldn't do anything immoral or wrong in my life—I feared the nuns would find me and there would be hell to pay. Lord, I was afraid of them! LOL! I was a good student and didn't give my parents any trouble. I babysat little ones from the time I was twelve years old. I am one of ten kids in my family. I have three older brothers, two older sisters, and four younger brothers. I had a lot of experience taking care of babies and littles. I had several families I babysat for on a regular basis when I was ages twelve to eighteen. I didn't go out on the weekends with my peers. That just wasn't me. I was ten in 1967 and observed my five older siblings tearing it up in the '60s lifestyle! They were into drinking and smoking marijuana and free "love." I remember my sisters got their hearts broken and some of their friends died in car wrecks, and so on. I just didn't want that for my life, so I stayed home.

Our family is very musical. We can all sing, and most of us play an instrument. My parents are marvelously talented. Dad was a plastering contractor by trade for over thirty-five years, and he worked very, very hard. He would come home, have a cold beer or two, fall asleep upright in a chair before dinner, and then after dinner, he would get out his 1955 Gibson Country and Western Jumbo guitar and play at the table while my two older sisters and I sang every country song you could think of. Truly, we were like a jukebox. This kept us from arguing while doing the dishes by hand for twelve people every single night! No mechanical dishwashers back then in our house—Dad said he had three of them! But music was a strong glue that bonded our large family together. My parents had several friends who had large families who would come over and "jam" with Dad and Mom, and we would sing and sing and sing.

If I had to describe my upbringing, it truly was like a Norman Rockwell painting. It was never easy, but it was home. My mother never had a lap. Seven loads of laundry every day—seven days a week. We were lucky enough to have an electric washer and dryer, but the outside lines were very important, too. Things needed to dry and keep those lines free for the next day's washing.

Mom was an excellent cook, and we always had a hot meal on the table at night. If she didn't have ten kids and years of work that never let up, my mom would have been on the stage and famous. She had, and still has at ninety-five, a Billie Holiday kind of voice. She loved jazz music. Dad was country music through and through. It coursed through his veins. They would sing together and harmonize so sweetly. We all learned the songs of four decades and how to harmonize through them.

In his forties, when I was a teenager, my dad went through a powerful spiritual awakening and abruptly left the Catholic religion. He was deeply convicted about his new beliefs, and this shook the very foundation of the family. I never questioned it much. I didn't question much that he ever did—he was my dad and I trusted him. I was about to leave home and while I knew there is a God, everything I had learned about Him throughout my childhood was through the filter of Catholicism. I knew nothing of other religions or spiritual beliefs. As an adult in my twenties, I had wandered around in the world exploring other religions and practices, I guess seeking my own Truth. I hadn't completely found that yet by the time I turned 30, but I did know that building a faith in my children was very important. I wanted them to learn to lean on what doesn't move, and this proved to be a good thing for them. I know it was for me.

So my kids and I started attending the Church of Christ in Conway. It was a small congregation of about seventy-five people, and we came to know them all over time. While the kids were in their Bible classes, I was upstairs in the adult classes. I came to know the Truth and became a Christian myself two months before Craig moved out. What a rocky road ahead for me, but it was the perfect time for me to grow my faith.

Although I didn't know what was coming, God did, and His timing is always perfect. That year would prove to be the greatest challenge of my life.

Kim and Debbie, the parents of that first little girl who came to my daycare in 1981, were some of the few who remained my friends during this time. Because I needed work, Kim offered me a job at the front desk of his family's motel. I couldn't get hired anywhere else. I was facing a jail sentence in April—who else was going to hire me? Kim and Debbie loved me and I knew it, so I jumped at that job. I worked from 3 p.m. to 11 p.m. five nights a week. Mom and Dad watched the kids for me. What would I ever have done without my mom and dad? They literally co-raised my littles.

I don't remember much about Jylian's first year of life. I don't remember much except the fears, the pains, the injustice of it all, month after month after month after month. I also cleaned houses and condos on the weekends during this time to keep food on the table. Craig struggled along with his own burden of loss, wrongful judgment, and ostracizing in his own life, but he maintained his financial support and visits with the kids. This was an absolute living hell for both of us.

I would have attacks of agoraphobia when I went grocery shopping. The person checking out my groceries wouldn't even look at me—never mind speak to me. When I tried to write out my check, I couldn't even see where I was writing. I could only hope it was correct because my vision was all fuzzy. Whenever I went to the bank, whether it was at the drive-through window or, God forbid, if I had to go inside, there would be two people in the corner whispering, "That's her. . . ." And people would stare and make snide remarks. Friends told me they had been at a party with the first psychologist involved in the case, and they had heard him discussing facts about the case and boasting about his knowledge. My sweet friend, Suzie, knew it was all lies. But the gossip would grow from these types of gatherings. Grow and grow and grow. I was drowning in a town in which everyone believed everything the newspapers printed. The media never got it right. After all, they were interested only in selling newspapers—not in getting the story straight.

Chiseling the Path…

Certain words we hear from others do permanent damage. A momentary wound with words can forever ache. Soon after the meeting with Mike and Sara, we had to attend an arraignment. Again, I thought we were just going to jail. I didn't know the first thing about trials, and it never occurred to me we might have one when we were served the indictments. But there we were, and the charges were read aloud to us.

I found myself standing there with Mike and Sara and just not believing the words coming out of that judge's mouth. Felonious sexual assault of two minors. I'm going to say this here, and it is a little embarrassing, but I was so naive that I didn't know what sexual abuse really meant. I asked my attorneys, "What are they saying we did?" I'm sure they can attest to that. I couldn't hurt a child if my life depended on it. Neither could Craig.

It paralyzed me when I first learned what these parents thought I did to their children. My relationship with the mother of A and B was a good one while the girls were in my care. She often asked me for advice about raising them and how to handle typical frustrations that all parents face. Her oldest didn't want to do dance and other activities she had enrolled her in. I thought maybe it was just too much at her young age and said not to push, maybe to just choose one thing she would like to do and stick with that. The younger child was eleven months old when she came to me, so just a baby. They fit in with the other kids just fine, and they were not any trouble.

Because we were separated and, actually, because we were two separate people, it was suggested that we have separate legal representation because if at some point we didn't agree on a process, the attorney would not be able to choose who to represent over the other party. One night early on, Craig came over to see the kids, and we were in the kitchen after they were put down for the night. Craig was sitting at the end of the counter, and I asked him what he thought we should do about having separate representation. He looked at me and said, "I know what I didn't do, but I don't know what you did or didn't do."

Like a sharp sword, those words ripped right through me. I have long forgiven that, and I know he wasn't in his right mind, but man, after being together twelve years and having two kids together… that one hurt deeply.

I want to point out something here. In all this time—two

years, in fact—I never had a voice. I never took the stand in a court of law; I never told my side of the story. I had to endure the newspaper articles, radio reporting, false accusations that would be fabricated and then retracted. I could say nothing. I wasn't ever able to speak to a reporter until the case was dropped and we called a press conference. Even on that one occasion, I was still robbed of that opportunity to set the record straight.

The local paper was invited to the scheduled press conference the morning after the charges were dropped. In typical newspaper fashion, they had to be first to announce the dropped charges, so the morning of the press conference, they had a full-page article with far too many misrepresentations and a grand lack of facts that made it an article of vindication. I was crushed and so incredibly angry. They were friends of ours, too.

I never had a voice. Never told my side of the story. How is that possibly FAIR??? Is there anything, anything at all that is fair about this whole ordeal? At this point, I was facing thirty-three years in prison. I was still walking around in shock and didn't understand half of what was being hurled at me in legal jargon. Day after day, night after night. I was having "friend" after "friend" turn their back on me because they were scared and didn't know what to believe. I was so afraid of our financial situation. Money wasn't coming in for either of us. How were we going to pay the bills? Was I really going to go to prison for something I didn't do? Was that true for both of us? Craig hadn't even known these kids.

Chapter Seven

Surviving Life's Crashing Waves…

The fear of facing a prison sentence lurked in and around every day, every holiday with my babies, every birthday celebration, Josh's first day of school. I literally spent every day trying to survive—all of it. Dr. Rabideau told me this was to be expected with the level of stress we were under, so he put me on medication. It helped some, but you still have to process it all.

From 1989 to 1991, Mike and Sara worked tirelessly to build our case against Paine, the prosecutor, for gross negligence as a prosecuting attorney. Our legal position against him was that he was grossly overstepping his role as a prosecutor and was acting as an advocate or investigator on behalf of the mother. This part of the case went all the way to the state Supreme Court to be decided. At the risk of opening Pandora's box and having a flood of lawsuits against prosecuting attorneys, they denied our case. Typically, you cannot sue the government. That position is technically one that represents the government side of a criminal case. We continued to sue both of the psychologists involved, Nagahiro and Harrison. Those lawsuits continued in court for the next eight years.

Craig chose to have Paul Hodes to represent him. He paid a $10,000 retainer to Paul, and Paul worked together with Mike and Sara. Paul was such a fun guy. He had the best sense of humor and, my favorite, was super sarcastic. He and his wife wrote and performed children's songs all over the area when he wasn't being a superhero lawyer in his "real job!" Mike had a cool hobby of making patchwork quilts when he wasn't lawyering. His softer side surprised me, because I knew him as my Columbo and such a ruffian! This was one of many times in my life that I realized the many facets of human beings. We are complex, amazing spirits with many gifts. I am thankful that the attorneys collaborated in our best interests. We needed all the support we could muster.

From age thirty to forty, I was in and out of courtrooms trying to prove my innocence and recover what we had lost financially. During this time, Harrison's attorney dropped dead in the shower, and in 1996, Bill Paine, the prosecutor, died in a hotel room traveling alone. Michael, my attorney, was hoping it wasn't a trend. I told him to take his vitamins! Once the charges were dropped on April 19, 1989, I physically went into a complete crash. I couldn't function and was in a terrible depression. I had not realized I had been physically functioning in a state of coping.

The Sculptor's Vision...

And now you will see the work of the Master. I had learned over these few years stories of others who were suffering through similar circumstances such as mine across the country. Some had their children taken from them. Some were arrested and spent time in jail. None of these things happened to Craig and me. We were sheltered from those atrocities, and God knew what and how much I could handle.

There were support groups that had formed around the country for those accused and caught in the web of injustice, but I honestly couldn't subscribe to that. I knew what I hadn't done, but I didn't know what any of the others may have done or not done. I didn't want to talk about it. I did everything in my power to try to live in a state of normalcy for Josh and JyI. They were already dealing with the pain and inconsistency of divorce. I had developed serious trust issues and felt truly alone in the experience. Remember, I felt like my hands were tied behind my back and that no one could really understand the level of humiliation I felt and endured while being completely innocent.

My brother Tom and his wife, Christine, had been such an integral part of this whole ordeal. He was a pillar of strength for me. He is a Vietnam veteran, and more than once he would tell me, "This is your Vietnam, Kath, this is your Vietnam." They lived nearby and became innkeepers at a beautiful, Victorian-style village in Jackson, New Hampshire, called Nestlenook Farm. It was a quaint, gorgeous property with horse-drawn sleigh rides in the winter and seven

Victorian guest rooms decorated like a fairytale!

One day, Tommy called me and asked me to come sing with him for the guests at the inn. I said, "Are you out of your mind? I haven't played the guitar in ten years." He said, "Eh, ask Mom to watch the kids and bring it up here. I've got lots of wine. The guests will never know the difference." So, come Friday night, I ventured up there, and we had an absolute ball with the guests. Tom played the guitar and I pretended to do the same. We sang so many songs they knew—and yup, the wine flowed! The room was downstairs in a beautifully finished cellar-walled recreation room. It was so warm and comfortable, and the guests knew they were part of something so sweet and special. We did this quite a few times with lots of new faces and just had such fun. And we were pretty darn good!

In the spring of 1990, Tom moved his family to Knoxville, Tennessee. He said to me, "You're never going to do anything with your singing, and you should." I let it drop and said, "You're crazy! Tom, I'm a single mother of two in Conway, New Hampshire. You have lost your mind."

After the charges were dropped in April 1989, I was determined to stay in my home and not move away because I was not guilty of the charges, and this was my home where my kids were growing up. My spirit is stubborn like that. I missed Tom and Christine so much after their move. They were determined to live in a milder climate and start fresh somewhere south. No one in our family had ever ventured south of the Massachusetts line. We were tried and true Yankees, as they say in the South. We knew no prejudice of any person, race, or creed where we grew up outside of

Boston. Tom and Christine were the adventurous kind in the family. Many followed their lead when they made these noble, drastic moves in their lives! Knoxville was the final decision, and it was a great one! Over the course of the next several years, five other family members made the same move to the Knoxville area, getting out of the snow and black-fly country!

Meanwhile, I was still in New Hampshire, and we had embarked upon our countersuits and were still in and out of court pretrial conferences, depositions, and all the rest. Every day, I was just begging for it to go away and allow me to get on with some sense of normalcy in my community. No such luck…

Not long after Tom and Christine moved to Knoxville, in October 1990, I was cleaning my house and heard about a competition on the radio that was happening in Portsmouth, New Hampshire. I thought, "I'll show him!"—it started as a complete dare—and I called about the competition. I learned it was through the Country Music Association of America. I could pay to enter into a category like female vocalist or band. I entered into the female vocalist category. I had never done anything like this. The date was set for me to go to Portsmouth to perform. Well, my parents were just thrilled to be a part of this. I would get six minutes to perform songs of my choice, and the competition committee would provide a backup band. My mom thought I should have a stage name—I think for obvious reasons—so I became Katie Belle! She penned the name, and I went with it! Going into the competition, I chose two songs and did my thing. It was quite competitive, with some really great talent. Well, I ended up winning the category. I called Tom and said, laughing, "Nah nah nah nah nah nah." He laughed and said, "I told you so!" Pay attention now.

I didn't know, as is characteristic of my personality, that because I had won in my category for the state of New Hampshire, I would have to go to the regionals and represent the state. Whaaa . . . ? So guess what happened then? The local papers got a hold of my win, and I was on the front page of the paper. They printed the whole story of the child abuse case and that I had won the competition. Then off to the regionals in Augusta, Maine, I went in January 1991. Nine Northeastern states competed in all the categories. Each contestant got six minutes, so I chose other songs, traveled to Portsmouth to rehearse and scared to death performed on behalf of the State of New Hampshire..

I was really shocked: I won the regionals, too! That time, less of the child abuse case was brought up on the front page of the newspapers, and more of the award winning was in the articles. I was becoming the hometown celebrity—the hero!

Once I won the regionals, I didn't know there were the nationals to contend with. Have you noticed I don't ask a lot of questions? LOL! Because I won the regionals, I now had an all-expense-paid trip to San Demas, California, to compete in the national competition. This included six regions in the U.S., including Nashville! I was a Boston-accented, country music-singing girl from New Hampshire with a crazy set of circumstances. The same protocol occurred at the nationals. I was singing on the same stage where Dolly Parton and Randy Travis had been entertaining the week before. The place seated 2,600 people in a dinner-club atmosphere. It was so surreal!

The End of the Line Band was my backup band, and I was going to sing two songs again, including "Don't Touch Me," which I learned from a recording made by Tammy Wynette. I was beyond nervous and excited at the same time. After the roller coaster of what seemed like an endless legal battle, these were new, different feelings. I surely didn't have any idea what or why this was happening, but I was rolling with it. It was required! My attorneys were also mystified as to what was happening here. Relatives and friends far and wide were getting wind through the grapevine of what was going on in my life now—God doesn't do anything small!

The funniest combination of family and friends followed me to California to witness the national competition. They were the best fans and supporters, and they also couldn't believe what was happening! I was so grateful to have them all there. It helped create a home environment and allowed me to just get up there and sing my heart out!

After seeing all the country's competition, I thought to myself, "This was a great ride, and there is no way I'm gonna win over her or her or her." Once we completed our performance, we were able to go into the seating area with our families and friends. I sat there as they called to the stage the winners of Band of the Year, Male Vocalist of the Year, and so many others, and then it came to the female vocalist category. Like it was out of a movie, I heard, "And the winner of the Female Vocalist of the Year category . . . Katie Belle!"

I had won the nationals! I couldn't feel my legs walking up to the stage to accept the award. I thought Tom was going to have a conniption fit! The award ceremony was followed by a celebratory dinner with our whole group and it was just the best time! I remember calling Mom and Dad on the phone from the hotel room and just hearing their whoops and laughter was something I will never forget!

I came home to Conway, New Hampshire, to front-page articles in newspapers all over. I had gone from wearing a Scarlet Letter to being the hometown celebrity. The phone began to ring now with inquiries to perform at this function and that resort. It was a whole different world! My hometown paper in Natick, Massachusetts wanted to do an interview for the *South Middlesex News* and so I did. People wanted my autograph and to hear me sing. That July 4th, in 1991, I stood with the Northeast Symphony as their featured vocalist on a huge stage in Schueller Park in North Conway in front of 10,000 of my accusers, singing Lee Greenwood's "God Bless the USA." God had literally turned an entire community on its head.

From that point forward, I was now a celebrity. The child abuse case was something in the past and brought up less and less in the papers. Can you even believe this? I know! It was absolutely surreal. I guess God had accomplished what He wanted to do through me and through Craig. As painstakingly awful as it was, He restored my honor. He vindicated us both.

And by the way, what was it that I said over and over during the criminal case? I had no what? No voice. And what was it that God used to turn our little town around for me during the worst time of my life? He used my voice, the gift He gave me.

Me and my mini-me at a photo shoot!

PHOTO BY BRUCE BEDFORD

'FAMILY VALUES' — Our own national champion country/western singer Katie Belle entertained at Schouler Park Thursday evening as part of Arts Jubilee's free 'Concert in the Valley.' She is shown here accompanied by her father, Tom Cormier, on a rhythm instrument. Belle credits her father with developing her interest in music and teaching her to sing and play.

The press could never get anything straight! This is my dad, but his name is George. Tom was my brother. Good grief…

Josh (5) and Jylian (18 mos)

Chapter Eight

As I began to share my story with others, I discovered that although the circumstances were always different from mine, many around me were navigating their own battles. Once again, my vulnerability created a safe space for others to share their experiences, leading to a powerful exchange of support and empathy, both of which I found myself offering to others, healing me in the process. Hence, my newfound nickname of "The White Oprah." Haha! I found solace in hearing how friends had overcome their challenges, which inspired me to see my own situation in a new light. Reframing vulnerability as a strength required a shift in mindset. I began to view it as an essential part of my personal growth and survival going forward. I reflected on how vulnerability allowed me to seek help, something I had previously resisted. Over the years, whether it was by reaching out to a mentor for career advice or confiding in a therapist about my mental health, these moments of openness were crucial for my healing.

Through this lens, I recognized that every time I chose to be vulnerable and transparent, I was taking a step toward authenticity. I learned to embrace my imperfections and accept that it's okay to not have everything figured out. This acceptance fostered resilience; I became more adaptable to change and open to new opportunities. When I faced setbacks—and there were some—I approached them with a mindset that acknowledged my vulnerabilities while also celebrating my strengths.

There is so much more to include here from the litigation side of what happened. I will need the help of my attorneys to pull those details together. It was a wild ride that they had never seen anything like before. There are no words to describe what those ten years took from me, took from Craig, and took from my parents. There are so many stories of others who were affected by the situation. How afraid I was to have Josh start kindergarten. I remember speaking with his teacher, Jackie, and asking her to please watch conversations around him to see if children were treating him wrong or telling him things about the charges. She was very good about it. We kept the kids sheltered from it all, and now that they are forty-one and thirty-eight, I think we did okay.

Dennis Harrison ended up losing his license and would never practice psychology again. He moved to Austin, Texas, became a so-called movie producer, created a Ponzi scheme, ripped off a number of investors, and was in the newspapers there. Who knows where he is today? I know the girls involved in the abuse allegations (A and B) went through some terrible times with their mother. During the mother's deposition, she admitted under oath that her older daughter had threatened to kill her. I have always been so sad for what those little girls were put through unnecessarily. During the criminal case, the father was asked to take a polygraph and failed. They said he had huge sweat rings under his arms and was freaked out to do it. We thought at that time, though, that it might have been somehow related to his time in the military. He later accused his wife of being crazy.

After ten years, we were forced to settle our countersuit for $650,000. We had sued for several million dollars. Every time you go into court, you run the risk of having the case thrown out. The judge may have had a fight with his wife that morning, and just through a knee-jerk reaction, he could throw out the whole case. If this were to happen, we would lose our opportunity to countersue for good. It was too risky to not take the offer from Harrison's attorneys in 1998 to settle.

Craig and I received a small portion of the settlement. The rest went to legal fees, which I'm sure didn't come close to covering the ten years of litigation and representation. That amount of money should have been millions for ten years of legal work and what we lost in income from our businesses, not to mention for our character assassination. I never owed Mike and Sara another dime. They became my family. I loved them as my eighth brother and third sister and was eternally grateful for their willingness and love.

I remember them encouraging me to write a book, write a book! I was afraid I could not possibly live through all that again at the time. They had a designated room full of file cabinets housing the thousands of legal documents associated with our case. Over countless hours, they had made countless trips to court and many other trips to piece together this nightmare.

The final day of stepping into that elevator on the seventeenth floor of their office building after saying goodbye to Mike and Sara was one of the hardest days of my life. They had been my safety net, my guardians and friends. I'm sure by the time we had met for the first time, Mike had been an attorney for a long time and thought he had seen it all. Well, not quite yet. He took a lot of heat for taking my case on and staying with it for so many years. I am also very grateful to his business partners in the firm. I know the firm was not properly compensated for all those years of work.

Through the litigation of this case, New Hampshire adopted a new law to prevent others from going through what we went through. That was a win. We played a part in uncovering a horrible ring of false accusations and false arrests all around the country and that deplorable underground railroad.

I learned to stand for my own Truth, which was the only Truth. We never did anything to harm a child. We both were as innocent as the day and were used for a greater purpose. It took many years to see that, but today I am grateful to be able to look back and see what was happening all along.

Above all, I grew, and I learned to lean on what doesn't move. God is real, and among all the evil we witness in this world, He has already established the victory. Again, we may not see it for many, many years. But this is also a Truth. We live in a human dimension where God has allowed there to be choice. Those who choose to do evil choose for themselves. Since not one of us is alone in this world, not one stands unconnected, we are sometimes subjected to the fallout or impact of that evil. It is the fallout of choice—not neglect from our loving God. This is sometimes a complex concept to understand, but life will prove it over and over.

Much of this time frame felt like I was crawling out of a deep, dark hole. You are probably wondering what happened once I won the national award with the CMAA! Well, there was quite a momentum built from the progression of winning the three consecutive awards. My brother, Tom, was as stunned about it all as he could be! By the time we got to the trip to San Demas, he and Christine, my sister-in-love, had to come and be a part of this process! He just couldn't believe what was happening! Remember… it all started as a ruse to answer his challenge that I would never do anything with my ability to sing, and how he said that it was a shame. LOL! I showed him! Or did I? Was it all in the hands of the Master Creator to redeem the last horrible years, to expose the truth about the case and allow me to stay in my home? Was it meant to turn the hearts of an entire community on its head? It would take something of this magnitude to do it, and that kind of power comes via only one Source in life!

Tom and my two other older brothers, Jim and Johnny, were in the music industry for nine years during the 1970s and part of the '80s. They had an awesome country rock band called Brothers Kingdom and traveled up and down the northeast coast playing venues, restaurants, and pubs.

As their lives changed with marriage and having babies, they disbanded and went into other careers.

Tommy had lots of connections in the music world, and he paid for me to come to Knoxville and lay down a pitch CD with Norbert Stovell at Big Mama Studios. Norbert recorded artists like Dolly Parton and such. He wasn't just a small-town recording studio! We were very happy with the recordings!

Tom was planning to present me and that pitch tape to the music world in Nashville and see where that might go. We pulled off that recording project of ten songs in three days. Norbert had some of the best and most talented studio musicians come in and make this album come alive. It was magic! That was amazing and exhausting!

As for Craig and me, our divorce was finalized, and we were still battling it out behind the scenes. Our moral structure and lifestyles were so diabolically different. As angry as I may have been at him, I never spoke disparagingly about him in front of the kids. Our arguments were not in front of them. Oh, they could feel the energy, I am certain, but I did what I could to spare them. I knew in my heart that in good times, as they matured, they would see the situation for themselves without any narrative from me. I also believe that no matter what the circumstances of divorce, he is still their father, and they need to have a healthy place to put that relationship for themselves and their development.

Meanwhile, in April—funny story! After I won the regionals, I wondered about writing my own music, so one night I was sitting in my den, playing the guitar, and I said to God, "Well, God, it has been four full years that I have been on my own, not even so much as a cup of coffee with a man, but I have been solely working on surviving financially and taking care of Josh and Jyl, and you know they are my life. Maybe you want me to be by myself the rest of my life. I will accept that and am grateful for all you have given me and how you have protected me and my family." Well, I took a piece of paper and pen and started writing. This song came out of me in fewer than thirty minutes—words, music—the whole tamale!

It was a song titled "Heaven, Can You Hear Me?" The lyrics were as follows:

> Hey, Heaven, can you hear me?
>
> I'm knockin' one more time
>
> My voice is no stranger
>
> Comin' over your line
>
> And this time when you hear me
>
> Please listen long and hard
>
> Cuz you ain't heard this one before
>
> It's special from my heart
>
> It seems like years that I've waited
>
> For the angel of my life
>
> I've been up and down and all around
>
> With love I thought was mine
>
> It's time I pray that you could see
>
> If I'm the next in line

Cuz I'm not busy, just sittin' pretty
Waitin' for my angel divine
Chorus
Heaven, Heaven, can you hear me?
Could you reach out on your line?
I'm prayin', prayin' for a baby
You're sure would suit me fine
Now, I'm not beggin'
But yes, I'm waitin'
For Heaven's winning prize
So send him down
To my little town
To love me all my life

Is that not crazy? I know, I know, it blew my mind! You'll see the final verse of this song later on. And would you believe . . . three weeks after writing this song, he showed up in church?

This church family was a very small congregation. Not many people traveled through, especially young, available men. We were introduced by the minister, and Brad asked me out on a date the next week. Brad came into my life just after winning the nationals, and things got serious very, very fast. We met in May and were married August 31 of that same year. He had two children from a prior marriage: Heather, nine, and Christopher, seven. I believe they were supposed to come into my life. More on that later.

I can honestly share that I really felt I had what it took to make it in the industry if I applied myself—except for the fact that I had two children whose father would not have agreed for me to take them on the road with me for 225 days a year. Although I am grateful for the wonderful love and experience of the competitions and local social transformation after the child abuse case, the music industry was not for me. It didn't resonate with who I am. I was far too concerned with how my children would turn out. I had to sheepishly explain that to Tom, who was gung-ho on launching my music career. He had invested in the albums and in me. I felt really terrible to let him down, but I had to be true to myself. Brad was new to the equation, so he didn't really weigh into that decision at this point. I just knew I was making the right choice.

I continued to sing within a two-hour proximity of home for nine years and made a good supplemental income from it. There was never a paid engagement where the crowd I played to was drinking and smoking. Quite the contrary. They were attentive and ready to have a great time! I had a long run with the bus tour industry who came through the White Mountains. I would entertain them for ninety minutes or so. I was home in my bed every night. It was perfectly designed—yet again!

I took Dad and Mom with me to many of my gigs and showcased them for all the talent they were. Dad had made a washtub bass and accompanied me with that. It was made of a large galvanized tub, a shovel handle, and a long piece of rawhide. He would make a joke during the show that the tub was their first bathtub to bathe their first five babies. The shovel handle was part of the shovel used to dig the first foundation of their house, and the rawhide was used to keep us all in line. Ha! Then he would tip the whole thing over, which exposed the empty galvanized tub, and tell the crowd it doubled as our tip jar if they were so inclined. He was a riot! Mom would come up and sing her rendition of Bill Bailey, and they would sing an old song called "Built in Love." The crowds ate that up like honey on a spoon! We would sing together for some songs, and the rest of the time I was carrying the crowd with sing-alongs, ballads, and stories! The whole experience was tailored to the person I am inside.

We were still deeply involved with the countersuit, and I was in and out of court over the next eight years. Craig did not go to any of the hearings or pretrial conferences or depositions. He would give his reason that he had to work, but I think it was that he couldn't handle it emotionally. It had taken everything from him in his mind, and it was impossible for him to accept.

Brad was in and out of court, fighting custody issues with his former wife, so we were no stranger to courtrooms and legal costs on his end. It was just miserable whenever those court dates came around. Heather and Chris lived with their mother, and every other weekend we would drive from Conway, New Hampshire, to Plattsburgh, New York, on Friday after work—nine hours round trip, keep them for the weekend, and drive back to Plattsburgh on Sunday—nine hours round-trip. We did this for five years, and I can attest we never missed a scheduled weekend. Sleet, snowstorms, hail didn't matter. We drove through the mountain notches and across Lake Champlain, with the ice breaker ahead of the ferry in the middle of the winter breaking up the ice to cross over to Plattsburgh. You could not dissuade Brad. You could have dissuaded me, by golly!

Shortly after Brad and I were married, he began to reveal things from his past that were really disturbing and not indicative of the character I thought I had married. However, you can't possibly know anyone in three months. I was head-over-heels in love with his heart. He taught adult Bible classes at church and knew the Bible backwards and forwards, chapter and verse. We became youth leaders and were there every time the doors opened. Over time, we led marriage enrichment classes for couples, and as far as I could tell, we were good in our marriage.

Brad had trouble holding down a job and would have bouts of severe depression and anger issues. I was not familiar with bipolar manic disorders, but boy, was I living with it. His daughter, Heather, came to live with us full-time when she turned twelve, while Christopher kept living with his mom in New York. Christopher would come back and forth for visits, but usually with great resistance. I was very concerned about the path toward which his life was headed with gangs and trouble in school. Josh was turning twelve and spreading his teenage wings as well. I had four teenagers all at one time. There aren't enough vitamins in all the world to sustain that level of insanity and health!

We had been married for ten years when, on Christmas Eve in 2000, Brad came into our room at four o'clock in the morning, turned on the light, sat on the edge of the bed, and told me he didn't love me anymore and wanted a divorce. I thought he was just having an "episode" and told him to come to bed, but he didn't and walked out of the room. I had seen a number of these episodes over the years, but he had never before said he wanted a divorce.

One day as I arrived home, he met me at the door in goggles and a pair of green mechanic overalls, with a Sawzall reciprocating saw in his hands. He had cut off the back of the house upstairs, clear across the second level. He said he was going to build a full dormer off the back and put a bathroom between the bedrooms upstairs. Y'all, I could see the garden from my bed—wide open spaces! By the way, he had never swung a hammer in his life.

He had gone to the library and taken out books on framing, electrical work, plumbing, and all the rest. He literally read the books and did the work. No pneumatic nailer for him—nope, he just swung a hammer. Each night, he would have horrible contraction cramps in his hands and arms—it was awful. He took six weeks off work to do this, with no pay coming in. He put large blue tarps over the roof to cover the gaping hole he made in the back of the house. When we had torrential rains one night, he woke up the kids at four in the morning and gave them broom handles to push up on the tarps to relieve the huge pockets of rain gathering in them. They were ready to burst and flow down the interior walls to the kitchen. Thankfully, with the kids' help, that disaster was averted by the grace of God.

Brad did build the dormer, spent money we didn't have, and blamed me for the whole ordeal, claiming I put him up to it. I didn't. Did we talk about someday doing that project? Sure—but not like this.

He had a brilliant mind. In the late 1990s, he had graduated *summa cum laude* from SUNY Plattsburg, top in his class in speech pathology. But episodes like the back of the house could happen at any time. With the advice of a builder from church and some help from sojourners there, the project was completed, and remarkably, he did a really good job.

Katie Belle top country music vocalist

Katie Belle, a.k.a. Kathy Belcher of Conway, was recently named National Country Music Female Vocalist of the Year by the Country Music Association of America at a national contest held in San Diemas, Calif. With that honor in hand she now hopes to land a recording contract. For more on the country & western singer, see Page 4.

(Tom Eastman/Mountain Ear Photo)

And here we go! This was winning the National Female Vocalist of the Year for the CMAA. The newspaper articles had a completely different twist as you can imagine!

New Hampshire Country Music Association female vocalist of 1990, Kathy Belcher, stage name, Katie Belle, displays her winning trophy in her East Conway home. (SCOTT ANDREWS PHOTO)

The ballad of Katie Belle

Conway woman top N.H. country vocalist

By Scott Andrews
Special to THE CONWAY DAILY SUN

It's Saturday night at Jackson's Nestlenook Inn. Guests are ushered into the small library for the evening's entertainment. A man steps forward. "I'd like to introduce Katie Belle, just last month named female vocalist of the year by the New Hampshire Country Music Association."

She stands and adjusts her guitar strap. Dressed in white cowboy boots and white dress, festooned with white fringe and brass buttons, she

see KATIE BELLE page 8

As God worked to restore our good names in the community, singing engagements kept rolling in as he used my voice, the one that was silenced for so long, to make that happen.

Page 2

Carroll Cou

It's on to Nashville for our Katy Belle

PHOTO BY FRANK GOSPODAREK

A WINNING SMILE is displayed by Kathy Belcher, who sings as Katy Bell, after her return home from becoming the Country Music Association of America's top female vocalist.

By FRANK GOSPODAREK

NORTH CONWAY — If you want to hear the best in country music, head for Nordic Village and Nestlenook Inn in Jackson beginning in June to catch Katy Bell, the Country Music Association of America's top female vocalist.

"I keep looking at the sky and ask, 'What's next there, Lord?' "

Kathy Belcher

Four lake a

By MARSHALL C. HEWITT

Two important meetings took place last week for Lakes Region residents concerned with the state's recent effort to expand public access to New Hampshire's lakes and rivers.

Tuesday, the five-town committee of representatives from communities surrounding Squam Lake met for the final time at the Holderness Town Hall, where the committee's report on possible access sites was presented to Darcy Bryant, an aide to Gov. Judd Gregg.

The following night, a multi-department panel under the Office of State Planning held a public information meeting at the Laconia City Library to hear input and explain its position on public access to New Hampshire's waters.

At both meetings, public sentiment ranged from concern over environmental impact to skepticism of the state's ability to provide funding for adequate maintenance and policing, given the current budget crisis in Concord.

Following a series of meetings that began in April after its formation, the Squam Lakes Selectmen's Conference on Public Access last week submitted its report to Gov. Gregg, naming four sites as possible areas to be developed for state-owned public access to Squam Lake.

Those sites include two that could handle up to 20 car-trailer units, one on the west end of Squam off Route 3 in Holderness, and the other on the east end off Bean Road in Moultonboro, part of the property belonging to State Rep. Allen R. Wiggin, who is also a Moultonboro selectman and a member of the committee.

Two other areas were identified for access to carry-in boats with parking for eight to 10 vehicles.

We'
S
w
usage witho

One of two s
the first with 80
with 100 feet
would be availal
end of the lake o
A fourth site
Sandwich at t
would also oper
craft such as can
The report c
mendation by t
the state "purch
struct, maintain,
sidize towns for
It also express
concern that in n
sion for develo
sites, the state s
zoning ordinance
The report al
problems of bu
size of water
removal of m
spreading aqu
qualified supervi
and water, which
power, should be
Along with
committee sent a
Gov. Gregg that
vironmental imp
mine at what poi
resulting from
would lead to d
lake.
It further stated
to the level of u
and that "uncont
not be the result o
Individual co
were even more d
thanked them o

Big Brothers

NOTICI

Oh, the Reba McIntyre fashion of the times!

Those earrings! Haha!

Page 8—THE CONWAY DAILY SUN, Thursday, December 13, 1990

Kathy Belcher chosen as best N.H. female country vocalist

KATIE BELLE

from page one

jokes about the outfit. "Got it the same store that Barbara Mandrell shops. The similarity between us stops there," she laughs.

"Let's start with an old country favorite of mine:

There's a storm across the valley,
The clouds are moving in...

She sings with a simple, free and easy manner, exuding confidence. Her eye catches others, one by one. She often winks and smiles. The audience joins for the chorus:

Feels so good to be back home again.
Sometimes this old farm
Seems like a long lost friend.
Lord it's good to be back home again.

She smiles and acknowledges the applause. Before starting her next song, she points out her parents in the corner of the room. "That's my Papa George playing washtub bass. Mama Lillian over there will be joining me on vocals.

"There's been a lot of bridges and dams," she continues. "I'm glad to say that just like in the song, Katie Belle's back home again."

And back in the news.

Kathy Belcher (Katie Belle is her stage name) is no stranger to the news. In October, 1987 she and husband Craig were indicted on sex abuse charges in a case arising from the day care center they ran from their East Conway home.

In April, 1989, the charges were dropped. This November, she and brought suit against Carroll Country attorney William Paine and two doctors in order to clear their names. "It is criminal that we had to live through this," she said.

Belcher is reluctant to discuss "the case" or "my hell of '87" as she calls it. "I want to put all that behind me," she says. "I'm looking only forward these days."

Last November 11, Kathy Belcher was named by the New Hampshire Country Music Association as female vocalist of the year. In January she plans to record some of brother Tom's songs. In February she will travel to Augusta, Maine, to compete for Colonial State Regional vocalist of the year.

"Yes, Kathy Belcher's been in the papers," she says. "But now it's Katie Belle who's making the news. Now God's decided to test me in a different way."

Katherine Cormier was born in Natick, Mass., the sixth of ten children and one of three girls. Her father George was a self-employed plastering contractor. Her mother Lillian, was a very busy housewife.

"My parents were both musical," she recalls. "Dad played guitar and sang. He knew every Buck Owens song there was. Mom used to sing with Dad and us kids."

George and Lillian recall that they'd have a family sing-a-long before putting the kids to bed. After the children were upstairs but before they were asleep, "we'd hear ten different voices, singing ten different tunes in ten different keys. It's a wonder anyone's ...

When my name was read as the winner, I must have been... simply dumbstruck... for I don't know how long. Then I felt my brothers pinching and poking me. 'Get up there!' they said. 'Kathy, you've won

—Kathy Belcher

ways dishes to wash — 12 place settings. "The three girls did the dishes," Kathy remembers. "Dad would get out and play his guitar and the four of us would sing all during the hour it took us to wash and dry the dishes."

For several years the three girls and parents performed locally in the Boston area, mostly at private functions in Knights of Columbus halls, doing variety, or as George called them, "minstrel shows" —songs, jokes and comedy skits.

The three oldest boys formed the country rock band Brothers' Kingdom which performed at the old Brothers II club on the North Conway strip. As a teen, Kathy sometimes performed with her brothers. Kathy moved to Mount Washington Valley permanently in 1977 with her husband-to-be Craig.

The family became scattered as the Cormier children married and formed families of their own. Craig and Kathy had two children, Josh, now eight and Jylian, four, both budding musicians.

Music remained a family affair from grandparents to grandchildren. "Music really is the bind that brings us all together."

when they announced the contest.

She entered for fun — and to hea[r] other singers in the state.

The judging was held in a privat[e] club in Dover. Belcher sang three song[s] including "Blue Bayou," an old classi[c] revived a few years ago by Lind[a] Ronstadt, and "Once A Day," a Conni[e] Smith tune she had sung with he[r] family as a child.

A few weeks later the contest promoter called and asked her to rehearse "Blue Bayou" for the awards night. Still she knew three other women had received similar requests.

The awards were presented at the Music Hall in Portsmouth, an old Victorian theater with red velvet drapes and an enormous proscenium. George, Lillian and all but one of the Cormier children were there. Tom couldn't attend.

With spouses, children and friends, the Cormiers took up three whole rows. The old music hall was filled to its capacity of a thousand. In addition to the contestants, Irlene Mandrell, a Hee Haw regular (and Barbara Mandrell's sister) were also on the bill.

There were three different competitions that I was honored to win. So, each one would have these types of articles. This one speaks of the child abuse case and then the award. I would be sick to my stomach when they did this. As time went on, making the reference to the case faded off.

Look Out, Loretta— Here Comes Katie!

CMA Honors Conway Woman As C&W Vocalist Of The Year

Things are looking up for Katie Belle (above), a.k.a. Kathy Belcher of Conway, who was recently named National Country Music Female Vocalist of the Year by the Country Music Association of America at a contest in San Diemas, Calif. Kathy hopes to cut a demo record in the next few weeks, and will then travel to Nashville, Tenn., in search of recording prospects.
(Tom Eastman/Mountain Ear Photo)

Move over Dolly and Reba—make way for Katie Belle!

Katie, the stage name of Conway resident Kathy Belcher, was recently named National Country Music Female Vocalist of the Year by the Country Music Association of America at a contest held in San Dimas, Calif., May 2.

Now, with the title in hand, she hopes to give her best shot to winning a recording contract in the country music capital of the world, Nashville, Tenn.

"I wanted the endorsement of the Country Music Association. I figure, if I'm going to do this, I'm going to do it right and not mess around in lounges singing for five years. That's just not me," Kathy said upon her return to Mt. Washington Valley last week.

Kathy plans to cut a demo tape in the next several weeks, and will then try to market it with record companies in Nashville in July, using some of the connections she has made through the contest.

She is also enlisting the help of one of her brothers, Tom Cormier, formerly of Mt. Washington Valley. Cormier, a booking agent for speakers for radio talk programs across the country, also has contacts in Nashville which Kathy hopes to utilize.

Tom, along with siblings Jim and John, used to sing in Mt. Washington Valley in the early 1970s in a band known as "Brothers Kingdom." Kathy, now 34, was too young to sing with the band on stage, but sang at home. Her mother, Lillian Cormier, taught the family how to sing harmony, and her father, George Cormier, played guitar.

Originally from Natick, Mass., Kathy has lived in Mt. Washington Valley for 12 years.

Tom reawakened Kathy's interest in singing two years ago by asking her to lay down a vocal track for a song he'd written. Entitled, "Christmas in the White Mountains," the tune was selected by Nordic Village and Nestlenook Farm owner Robert Cyr of Jackson as a radio advertising theme song during the holiday season.

"That was the first time I'd ever done any recording, but that was it. The guitar came out of the closet after being put away for 10 years, and I've been at it ever since," she beamed.

Tom urged her to enter the contest last year after Kathy heard about it on WOKQ-FM. "Tommy said to go for it. It started out as a joke, really, but I wanted to see what talent was out there," she said.

Kathy's quest for the country female vocalist of the year title began last September, when she won the state title in Portsmouth.

She then competed against singers from throughout the Northeast last February at a contest in Augusta, Maine, to win the

SINGER continued on Page 6

I didn't know what was happening, honestly, the whole music thing began as a ruse between my brother and me. God used it for a much greater cause!

Here I am today holding all three honors that played such an integral part of redeeming so much loss in my life.

Performing at the Nationals in San Demas, California!

After winning the State of New Hampshire Female Vocalist of the Year.

Performing at the State of New Hampshire award show.

Winning the State of New Hampshire Country Music Association of America Female Vocalist Award 1991. Also, my very funny friends (Susie and Corinne) creating the Homes of the Stars Tour! My daughter, Jylian, just four years old here wondering what was happening with Mom!

Chapter Nine

It was Christmas in 2000. After Brad's announcement that he wanted a divorce, you can imagine how the day went for the four kids. He would steal the joy out of every holiday. He would sabotage anything and everything we tried to do as a family, and if he got into one of his moods, there was hell to pay for the day. I didn't let him get away with it and would have a major argument with him away from the kids. It would always end with him coming to me to apologize, but everything would just cycle again and again.

After Brad said he wanted a divorce, I proceeded to find out that he had been having affairs throughout our marriage. His behavior over those years appeared to me to be sociopathic and narcissistic. He could just shut off whatever was going on outside our marriage when he was with me, and I guess he shut me off when he was with the other women. For over a year, he had been carrying on with a teacher at a school where he was conducting preschool speech therapy. She was married to a police officer in Conway. It was the ugliest thing to have all that come out, and in the way he did it. Just horrible. He literally yanked the heart out of my chest. And how did I find out? As God would have it . . . See, I have learned through my life that yes, bad things happen—but are they really bad? We label everything good and bad, but must we? Is there not good that comes out of every hardship? I believe it. Even though I have had to suffer through some things that didn't seem to belong to my life. I believe God will call us out of circumstances that He can see from a much broader view. As he calls us, pulls us from the circumstances, it hurts because thread by thread, we are unraveling a life that was woven together.

I have a dear friend, Betsy, who is a cosmetologist and lives in a sleepy little Maine town on the New Hampshire border. As it happened, one day a customer came in for a haircut and they got to talking, as hairdressers and clients do all the time! This client had been having a difficult time in her marriage with her husband's infidelity, and she told Betsy that although married, she had found someone and was involved with him. Betsy asked his name and about dropped her scissors when the woman told her. Betsy's mom and dad were like surrogate parents and very close friends with Brad and me. We all went to church together as well. Betsy went to her mom and told her what she knew. They had the painful task of telling me the news and wondered whether they should. Well, they did, and the few truths about my ten-year marriage started to come out.

I remember standing at the refrigerator of Betsy's mom, Jane, holding the handle, crying so deeply and struggling to take a breath. Jane stood in front of me, saying, "Breathe, Kathy, breathe!" The pain was so incredibly deep into my heart that it was struggling to come out. Doing so kept me from breathing, and for some time that day.

I had given myself fully to Brad. I had lost myself in that marriage because the years with four teenagers and him were so awfully demanding. Those are difficult years in the best of circumstances, and ours, being a blended family, presented struggle after struggle with former spouses, kids pushing boundaries, and now trying to re-identify myself and stumbling to find the road to healing and singleness once again. When would my life find a peaceful road? If there's anything lonelier than being single, it's being single again.

Navigating these waters are some of the toughest in the human experience. When a spouse dies, it is extremely difficult, but it is also different from the loss from a divorce. After a divorce, your spouse is still on the planet somewhere, but he doesn't want to be with you. At one point, you were bound together for the duration of both of your lives here on the earth. Marriage is a sacred vow. The tearing apart is so painful, and we need someone or several people who can uphold the state of strength we need to work through it. My sister, Joan, was that for me. I cannot convey into words what it meant for me through so many of these really hard years that I could call her, and after her "Hello" go silent—nothing could be heard except for deep, choking sobs where words do not exist. She would say to me, "It's okay; just let it all out." And I would cry on the other end of that phone while my head and heart worked together to sweep this pain, disappointment, and disbelief from the core of my being.

Joan was so important to me through that time, and I am eternally grateful to her for that. She knew to not say too much and sometimes to say nothing. She just knew. She is six years older than me, and after growing up together, the nature of our relationship changed shape over the years. Growing up together means sharing a unique language of experiences—inside jokes, shared dreams, and the collective understanding of family dynamics. This familiarity creates a safe space in which both siblings can express their emotions freely. I knew Joan would always listen and offer support without reservation.

As I said, I knew Brad had depression issues, but I had no idea about his affairs. I had no clue when he would have had the time to be unfaithful! We spoke on the phone multiple times every day. I had vowed to never be a watchdog kind of wife. I would trust my husband and pray he was trustworthy. After he left and I looked back over our time together, I could recollect times that were suspect.

During each of my performances, I had told my story about writing that song and meeting Brad. After my heart was broken, I stopped telling the story. I was betrayed, fooled, disappointed, and furious to realize how much I had sacrificed for him. I lost all sense of trust.

We were formally divorced in May 2001. Christopher, Brad's son, asked me, "Kathy, what happens to us now as a family?" He knew that if Brad and I divorced, it would detach us as well. I told Christopher that law does not dictate love. He and Heather would always be my kids, and they would always be part of our family. Heather was eighteen, and Christopher was sixteen and headed for the

Army soon. They both have loved our continued relationship over these twenty-plus years. They are in touch regularly, we spend our holidays together, and they come and go with visits. Ultimately, I believe a huge reason my marriage to Brad happened was to connect Christopher and Heather to me as a support person in their lives. I take my role seriously.

Each of us has a story to tell. It's part of the human experience. Have you ever stopped to ponder the fact that we are a spiritual being that comes into the human experience for a time, and then we return to spirit after this life here on Earth? Do you ever wonder, in your quiet drives in the country or in the depths of despair and loss, "What is the purpose of life? What does it all mean?" I have wondered this since I was probably ten years old. I remember praying to "God" routinely when I was a child, but my first, most vivid memory of doing so and feeling some connection to Spirit, God, or an unseen power greater than myself was when my brother Tommy went to Vietnam.

As a kid of just thirteen, I didn't really understand war and the grave danger Tommy was in, but I remember praying and weeping and begging for God to bring him home safely. He was on the front lines as a Marine for thirteen months. I noticed my mom and dad were anxious about his being there, hanging on every letter that came in the mail and the very few phone calls we got from him. The phone line would sound like it was underwater while we asked too many questions to answer, but the most important one was, "When are you coming home?"

I remember making promises to God that if He would just bring Tommy home, I would stop doing this or that, or I would help more around the house, or . . . or . . . or. The day Tommy came home, he came to the back door after Mom and Dad picked him up at the airport. He was as thin as a rake—135 pounds if I remember correctly. He smoked cigarettes and reflexively used outrageous language and was constantly apologizing for it. He had witnessed hell on this earth. He has witnessed the most evil atrocities known to man and was now expected to come home and just rejoin society like nothing had ever happened.

I later witnessed the same thing through my bonus son, Christopher. He was one of the first on the ground after 9/11 in Iraq. If I remember correctly, he turned nineteen and twenty on the streets of Baghdad and Fallugia. He saw the statue of Saddam Hussein come down and was subjected to much of the same savagery and the horrible behavior of an evil capability in mankind.

There is so much to say about this, but that will have to be another book. I can tell you in both instances, both as a sister and as a mom figure, they were the most heart-wrenching days and yet also a time of great faith building, like other times of my life. There is truth to that statement. With every experience you and I have in our lives, we tend to label it good or bad. But is it really one or the other? Time will soften the most difficult challenges to a place where we can see them through a different perspective or lens and see the "silver lining" or the promise of the following:

> Romans 8:28: "And we know that in all things God works for the good of those who love him, who have been called according to his purpose."

Could it be that our labeled failures are merely feedback? I've learned that our failures are exactly that. We are able to see what happened and hopefully learn what the lesson was for us and how to adjust in the future.

Have you ever noticed that the right person or the right article, billboard, or phone call seems to just "show up" at just the right time to provide an answer, a thought with direction, or something else useful? I can speak to that personally. I have experienced such occurrences in every area of my life.

Chapter Ten

So my goodness, what is happening today, this many years later? I wonder: Can you answer the question for me? "Heaven, Can You Hear Me?" Did Heaven hear? Where do you see His hand move in the circumstances, situations, and conditions of my story?

All these extraordinary situations have led me to an extraordinary career in transformational life coaching. Long overdue! I now teach others how to co-create the life they would love. To dream big and impact the world for good. To forgive on levels we need to release our own hearts from the bondage of lack, depression, anger, anxiety, and lifelessness. To learn to follow the still, small voice that is speaking to you every day, as loudly as you are willing to hear it, toward a life full of abundance!

And so here it is: The final verse of the song, "Heaven, Can You Hear Me?" It goes like this . . .

> I can see him now with my eyes closed
> He's every mama's pride

Dreamy eyes that know where to look
When he's not by my side
The wisdom of the ages
Respect in every word
Hey, Heaven, if you hear me
Send down my just reward
Chorus
Heaven, heaven, can you hear me?
Can you reach out on your line?
I'm praying, praying for a baby
You're sure will suit me fine
Now, I'm not begging
But yes, I'm waiting
On Heaven's winning prize
So send him down
To my little town
To love me all my life!

Although I previously thought I had completed the song, "Heaven, Can You Hear Me?" I felt the last verse needed to become part of this passage of my life. See, it is now part of my life's vision, appearing in the love and relationship quadrant of my life. I'm excited to see how it plays out!

As I stand at the threshold of this chapter in my life, I am filled with a profound sense of gratitude. Looking back, I see a tapestry woven with threads of faith, resilience, and hope—a reminder of the journey I have traveled this far through the valleys of adversity. It is here, in the delicate balance of struggle and growth, that I have found my true self.

In those moments of doubt, when the shadows crept in, I

leaned into my faith. It became a sanctuary where I could lay down my burdens and find solace, not all the time—in all honesty—but many times. Now, I love to stare at the stars on a dark night, feeling the vastness of the universe around me and realizing that my struggles were but a small part of a much larger narrative. With each breath, I feel the weight of my worries begin to lift, replaced by a sense of peace that transcends understanding. When my voice is lifted in song and my gift is used to reach others, it is with deep thanks that I believe "Heaven, Can Hear Me?" has played itself out. Indeed, Heaven heard. Heaven heard me.

Acknowledgements

To my sister-in-love, Christine Cormier who helped with creating this meaningful cover, thank you so much!

To my niece, Kim Tuttle, and her beautiful artwork lovingly gifted to the Dedication page. Thank you, Kim, it is so special to me!

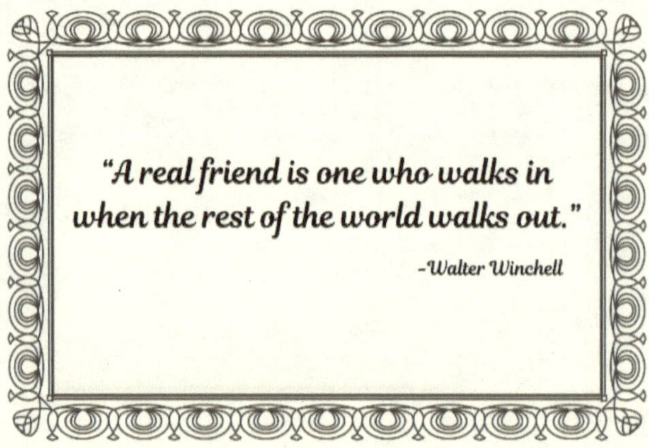

About the Author

Kathryn Cormier is a Transformational Life Coach and Mega-Producer Realtor. She resides in Knoxville, TN. Her passion is coaching people to live the life they would love! She is an award-winning vocalist, author, Mom and Nana, an entrepreneur, loves God and is ever grateful for this gift we call life.

Here we are today! My heart, my life's co-pilots. (Left to right) Josh, Jylian, Me, Heather & Chris.

My life's treasures! 7 beautiful, amazing creatures I get to call grandchildren. Blessings come as joy in the morning.

Hey, Heaven Can You Hear Me?

Please scan this QR code and enjoy the recorded song!
This is a thank you for reading my story. I hope it has blessed your life.

www.ingramcontent.com/pod-product-compliance
Lightning Source LLC
LaVergne TN
LVHW051008080826
845145LV00009B/2517

* 9 7 8 1 9 6 8 8 3 0 0 8 3 *